MW00569224

# SEARCHING
## *for*
# WATERCRESS

*First Published in USA 2006 by Rose Marie Bratek*

*Copyright © Rose Marie Bratek, 2006*

*All rights reserved. No part of this book may be reproduced or transmitted
in any form or by any means, electronic or mechanical, including
photocopying, recording, or by any information strorage and retrieval system,
without prior written permission from the publisher.*

*Manufactured by*

**FRP**™

*P.O. Box 305142*
*Nashville, Tennessee 37230*
*1 (800) 358-0560*

*Book Design, Food Prep, Styling and Photography by Rose Marie Bratek*
*Photographs accompanying storyline by Gene and Rose Marie Bratek*
*Recipes edited by Sally McNeill, RD, Nutritionist*
*Recipes are author's versions of favorite recipes,*
*which are not necessarily original.*

*ISBN 0-9786635-1-9*
*Printed in China*

# SEARCHING *for* WATERCRESS

•

## A MEMOIR COOKBOOK
### *by Rose Marie Bratek*

•

*A 40-Year Food Journey*

*From New Bride, New Cook*

*To Hostess and Headmaster's Wife*

•

*Favorite Food Stories, Memories*

*Recipes & Photographs*

•

*Salami and Watercress Hors d'oeurves*

4

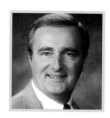

*The rather odd title for this cookbook came to me as I was thinking about the dedication. There was never any question that it would be dedicated to Gene, my husband of forty years, who was always willing to help me in any way he could, short of cooking that is. The "watercress story" says it all.*

*The year was 1967. Preparations were underway for our first cocktail party and all was going reasonably well until I read the recipe for the Salami and Watercress Hors d'oeurves. I had no watercress. I panicked. "Not to worry," Gene said, and off he went. Several hours and many, many stores later he returned with the watercress. Gene knew my perfectionist tendencies would not allow this party to go on without that watercress. Of course, years later I realized that any dark green, curly-edged lettuce would have been fine, but at the time I was striving for perfection. No substitutions would do. And to be perfectly honest, I just didn't know any better.*

*The search for watercress, therefore, became the perfect metaphor for my search for success in the kitchen. Preparing the right combination of foods for a meal; finding the correct timing for everything to be ready at the same time; creating the most eye-appealing and healthy recipes; all takes time and experience. The search would take a lifetime, but with Gene's encouragement and good humor, learning to cook was fun and relatively painless. Recipes were modified to our tastes and food stories were seasoned as well. The memories, photographs and recipes appear in this book.*

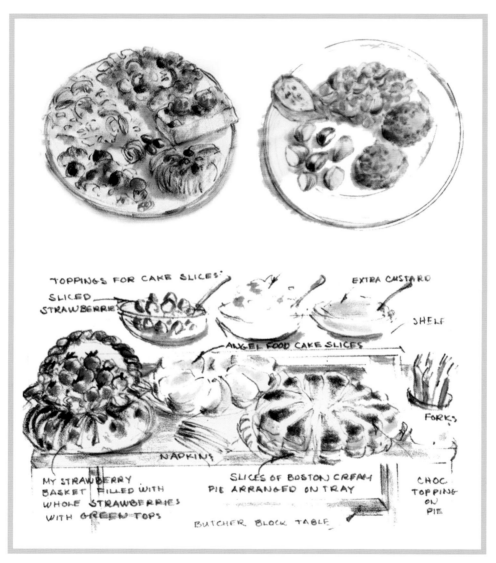

Party Planning Sketches

*Although* I toyed with the idea of creating a cookbook for many years, it was my son Jim who really encouraged me to get started. As a fellow graphic designer, Jim felt it was something I really should do. "A well-designed cookbook is always a welcome addition to any cook's library," he said. And I think having the recipes that he enjoyed growing up was at least part of his motivation for encouraging me. He and his wife Tara love to make these family recipes in their home as well.

*I* am grateful to my mother Helen Millus and my late mother-in-law Corrie Bratek for passing along old family recipes and also for their guidance and tips in the kitchen.

*Thanks* also to other family members and friends whose recipes are included in the book.

# CONTENTS

The Early years:
*Learning To Cook*
10

New Baby, New Country:
*Cooking In Germany*
28

Toddler Time:
*Getting a Toddler To Eat*
40

My Moms and Me:
*Recording Family Recipes*
58

Headmaster's Wife:
*Organizing Parties*
80

Headmaster's House:
*Planning Breakfasts, Luncheons & Dinners*
100

*Having Fun With Theme Parties*
133

The Later Years:
*Learning Never Ends*
162

Index
165

THE · EARLY · YEARS

*I* **never cooked before I was married.** *After arriving in Charlottesville and settling into our ivy-covered cottage on Rugby Avenue, I found a little cookbook tucked away with a wedding gift of stainless steel pots and pans. The recipes were simple, easy-to-follow, with just a few ingredients, not intimidating at all. "Bride's Dinner"(next page) is based on a recipe from that cookbook. I gained confidence by trying new recipes, inviting friends to dinner and having great fun in the process.*

Pictured below, clockwise from upper left: Baked Apple, Mashed Sweet Potato Cup and Pork Tenderloin Slices.

❖ *Bride's Dinner* ❖

# BRIDE'S DINNER

*In the original recipe, the pork chops, apples and sweet potatoes are baked together in one casserole dish, but in the forty-five minutes required for the apples to bake, the pork chops are often dry and the sweet potatoes are overcooked. I now substitute a pork tenderloin for the pork chops and brown it on top of the stove. I bake the apples in the oven and prepare the sweet potatoes in the microwave.*

2 medium-sized apples, Rome or
  Fuji
2 tablespoons seedless raisins
1 tablespoon brown sugar
¼ teaspoon cinnamon
1 tablespoon butter
2 tablespoons honey

1 tablespoon canola or light olive oil
1 pork tenderloin
2 medium-sized sweet potatoes
1 tablespoon butter
1 tablespoon sour cream
1 tablespoon chopped green onion

Preheat oven to 400 degrees. Wash and dry apples; remove the cores. Fill with the raisins that have been tossed with the sugar and cinnamon and place in a large oven-proof casserole dish. Top the stuffed apples with the butter and drizzle a tablespoon of honey over each apple. Add ¼ cup of water to the casserole dish and bake for 45 minutes.

Heat oil in a skillet and brown tenderloin on all sides. This should take about 15 minutes. Insert a meat thermometer into the thickest part of the tenderloin and place meat in the casserole dish with the apples for their last 10 minutes of baking time. Pork should be cooked to 155 degrees on the meat thermometer. While the apples are baking and the pork is browning, wash the sweet potatoes under running water and blot with paper towels.

*Continued on page 14.*

## "Company coming? No problem. I'll make a duck."

### FIVE PEOPLE, ONE DUCK

*After I managed to cook a couple of successful meals, Gene suggested that we invite a few of his fraternity brothers for dinner. "Great," I said excitedly. "I'll make a duck!" "Have you ever made a duck?" Gene ventured warily. "No, but there's a recipe in my little cookbook…not a problem." What I didn't realize at the time is that a four or five pound duck reduces in size considerably as it roasts and the fat is rendered. Five hungry adults sat down at the dinner table that night to feast on one very tiny duck. Our three large-sized guests picked the bones clean and left pretty quickly. They probably headed to the nearest pizza parlor to get some food! Duck recipe appears on opposite page.*

*Bride's Dinner continued from page 13.*

Prick the sweet potatoes in several places and microwave on high for 2 minutes. Turn potatoes over and microwave for an additional 2 minutes on high. Remove and wrap in a tea towel and let them rest for about 5 minutes. If the potatoes are still too firm, microwave another minute or so until tender. Cut each potato in half and stand on the pointed edge side. You may have to cut off a little of the point in order for the potato to stand on end.

Scoop out the sweet potato pulp to within a quarter inch of the sides and bottom. Mash the pulp with the butter and sour cream; stir in the chopped green onion.

Reheat the mashed potato pulp in the microwave one minute and divide evenly among the four scooped-out shells. Keep warm.

To serve, slice the pork tenderloin and arrange on two pretty plates. On each plate, place one baked apple and two sweet potato halves. Serve with a green vegetable of your choice. Light the candles. Serves two newlyweds.

## ❖ *Roast Duck* ❖

4-5 pound duck
½ teaspoon salt

**Orange Sauce** (optional):
1½ tablespoons butter
2 tablespoons flour
¾ cup beef stock, heated
¼ teaspoon paprika
1 tablespoon grated orange rind
½ cup hot orange juice (juice of one
    orange)
1 tablespoon sherry

Preheat oven to 325 degrees. Wash and dry the duck, removing the packet of gizzards and the neck first. Rub duck inside and out with the salt. Place breast side up on a rack in an open roasting pan. Do not add water. Roast for 2½ to 3 hours or about 40 minutes per pound. Serves 3-4.

To prepare sauce, melt butter in a small saucepan. Stir in flour and brown slightly; add hot stock and paprika, stirring until thickened. Just before serving, stir in rind, hot orange juice and sherry. Yields one cup.

# ❖ Coq au Vin ❖

*Because of the long list of ingredients, which in the early years intimidated me, it took some time before I tried this recipe. One try was all it took for us to enjoy this classic chicken dish over and over again. The wonderful aromas of the bacon and chicken browning along with the simmering bouquet of herbs and sherry make this recipe a particular favorite for dinner parties. Your guests will be welcomed at the door with these wonderful aromas coming from the kitchen. "Oh that smells so good," is the likely response you will get. But they'll like it even more when they taste it.*

*In the original recipe, a whole cut-up chicken was used, but this can be rather messy to eat since the chicken pieces are dripping with this incredibly tasty sauce. I substitute drumsticks and boneless chicken breasts for a nice combination of white and dark meat. Recipe appears on opposite page.*

*"Gene, we didn't have any sherry, so I used the bottle of Cherry Herring instead."*

*We toasted the best Coq au Vin dinner we ever had!*

## COQ AU VIN

2 whole boneless chicken breasts
4 chicken drumsticks
2 tablespoons unsalted butter
$\frac{1}{4}$ pound bacon, cut into pieces
$\frac{1}{2}$ cup sliced onions
1 clove garlic, minced
2 tablespoons chopped fresh parsley
1 teaspoon dried marjoram
1 bay leaf
$\frac{1}{2}$ teaspoon dried thyme
$\frac{1}{2}$ teaspoon salt
2 cups sherry
1 tablespoon cornstarch
$\frac{1}{4}$ cup carrots, sliced on the diagonal
$\frac{1}{2}$ pound mushrooms, halved

Preheat oven to 350 degrees. Cut chicken breasts in half, then each half into three pieces. Brown the chicken pieces and drumsticks in butter and bacon, then transfer to a shallow, oven-proof casserole dish.

To prepare the sauce, pour off most of the drippings from the skillet and sauté the onions until they are soft and translucent. Add the garlic and seasonings along with the sherry and using a wooden spoon scrape up the browned bits from the bottom of the skillet. While the sauce is simmering, mix the cornstarch with about two tablespoons of water, then stir slowly into the sauce. Continue to stir until sauce thickens. Pour the sauce over the chicken and bake for 30 minutes. Add mushrooms to casserole for the last 10 minutes of baking time. Serve over rice. Yields 4 servings.

For a quick, flavorful rice: Saute about $\frac{1}{2}$ cup of chopped onions in 2 tablespoons of unsalted butter until the onions are soft and translucent. Stir in one cup of raw rice, add 2 cups of chicken broth and bring to a boil. Turn down heat and simmer rice, covered, for 30 minutes.

❖

*"What is it?"*

was not the
response I was
looking for when
I proudly served
Gene my first squash
dish. "It's the squash
you wanted," I answered as I
started to cry. Of course he was
expecting the fried version that his
Southern-born mother used to make.
I prepared a squash recipe from my
red-and-white basic cookbook entitled
"zucchini on a half shell". What did
I know; I never even ate squash. Gene
did eat the squash I cooked, but ever
since that day we refer to the recipe
as "squash canoes".

Not long after that tearful episode, I
wisely called my mother-in-law for
instructions to make the southern-
style fried squash that we both enjoy
today. The recipes for both versions of
squash appear on this page. A squash
canoe is pictured above; fried squash
on the opposite page.

## SQUASH CANOES

To make Stuffed Squash: Cut two squash in
half lengthwise and brown, cut side down, in
a buttered frying pan. Turn squash over, add
two tablespoons of water, cover and steam
for 10 minutes or until tender. Scoop out
soft centers and fill with taco mixture. To
make the Taco Filling: Saute $\frac{1}{4}$ cup each of
chopped onion and red pepper until tender. Add $\frac{1}{2}$
pound ground beef and cook until browned. Add
$\frac{1}{4}$ cup each of canned corn, chopped black olives
and salsa. Season with $\frac{1}{2}$ teaspoon each of ground
cumin and chili powder. Salt and pepper to taste.
Divide filling among 4 squash halves. Serves 2.

## SOUTHERN FRIED SQUASH

2 medium-sized zucchini or yellow squash
2 tablespoons all-purpose flour
Salt and pepper to taste
4-5 tablespoons cooking oil

Wash the squash and pat dry with paper tow-
els. Slice cross-wise into $\frac{1}{4}$-inch slices. Place the
flour, salt and pepper in a plastic bag. Add squash
slices and toss to coat lightly. Heat oil in a heavy
skillet to medium-high heat and fry the floured
slices in one layer. Turn slices to brown both
sides, then transfer to a paper towel-lined plate to
blot excess oil. Serves two as a side dish.

❖ *Southern Fried Squash* ❖

❖ *Beef Stew* ❖

## "*Simmer for two hours?*
## *But we're hungry now!*"

## BEEF STEW

*The first time I made Beef Stew I gathered all the ingredients together and followed the recipe until I got to the part that read, "Cover and cook for two hours." "Why didn't they tell me that in the beginning," I cried. I was tired; we were both hungry. There was no way we were waiting 2 hours to eat dinner. The beef stew would have to be tomorrow's dinner. That day a quick sandwich would have to do. I learned a valuable lesson. Be sure to read the complete recipe well in advance of preparing it.*

$1\frac{1}{2}$ pounds beef, chuck or round
$\frac{1}{3}$ cup flour
$\frac{1}{4}$ teaspoon pepper
$\frac{1}{2}$ teaspoon salt
3 tablespoons oil
$\frac{1}{4}$ cup diced onion
1 clove garlic, minced
$2\frac{3}{4}$ cups boiling water
1 can (14.5 ounces) tomatoes
$\frac{1}{2}$ teaspoon salt
$\frac{1}{2}$ teaspoon Worcestershire Sauce

3-4 medium potatoes, peeled, quartered
12 small white onions, peeled
12 baby carrots
1 cup frozen peas

Trim fat from meat and cut into $1\frac{1}{2}$-inch cubes. Combine flour, pepper and salt in a plastic bag; add meat cubes and shake until all pieces are coated lightly. Heat oil in a large heavy skillet; add meat and brown on all sides. Add the diced onion, minced garlic, boiling water, canned tomatoes, salt and Worcestershire Sauce. Cover, reduce heat to low and simmer for two hours or until meat is tender.

Add the potatoes, small white onions and carrots; cook for twenty minutes. Add peas and cook for 15 minutes longer. Serves four.

Note: A great crusty, Artisan bread goes well with beef stew to sop up all that delicious gravy.

*Pictured below: Tuna and Bologna Roll-ups.*

❖ *Party Hors d'oeuvres* ❖

# FIRST COCKTAIL PARTY

*Salami-Watercress Hors d'oeuvres*

*The idea for having a cocktail party came to mind soon after Gene and I moved from Charlottesville to a new apartment in Piscataway, New Jersey. We were settling into our jobs. Gene was an American history teacher at Rutgers Preparatory School and I was a graphic designer for a local advertising studio. I had been clipping recipes from the food pages of magazines and I was fascinated with the colors and shapes of different finger sandwiches and party foods. Out went the invitations, in came the family and friends and our first cocktail party was underway. Despite a few first-party glitches (see "the watercress story" on page 5) a good time was had by all. Most importantly for me, it was a learning experience. Knowing how to prepare food for a large group would prove invaluable in later years when we hosted parties at our future schools. A selection of some simple hors d'oeuvre recipes starts on the next page.*

*Pictured left to right: Tuna Roll-ups, Bologna Roll-ups, Bologna Triangles, Salmon & Cucumber Stacks.*

## Tuna Roll-ups

*Use a firm white sandwich bread for best results. Chopping the filling in a food processor is easiest, but you can mince the celery, onion and tuna by hand and toss with the mayonnaise and mustard. Any spread, such as flavored cream cheese or your favorite filling, can be substituted for the tuna filling. The number of servings will vary according to how thickly the filling is spread on the flattened bread slices. (Make an assortment of different recipes and shapes to make an attractive party tray.)*

¹/₄ cup each chopped celery and green onion
6-ounce can tuna, drained
1 teaspoon Dijon mustard
¹/₃ to ¹/₂ cup mayonnaise
10-12 slices white sandwich bread
Green or black olive slices or pimiento pieces, for topping

Process chopped celery and green onion briefly until a fine mince. Add tuna and process a few seconds more. Add mustard and mayonnaise and pulse on and off until thoroughly mixed.

Trim crusts from bread slices. To flatten the slices, moisten a clean tea towel and lay it across a chopping board. Place two slices of bread on upper half of the towel. Fold the remaining half of the towel over the slices. With a rolling pin, roll to flatten the bread. Spread a tablespoon of tuna filling on each flattened bread slice. Roll up each tuna-spread bread slice tightly and wrap in plastic wrap; refrigerate for several hours or overnight until firm. Repeat with remaining bread slices and filling. To serve, cut each roll into 3 or 4 pieces, top with an olive slice or pimiento piece and arrange on a tray. Ten tuna roll-ups, cut into 4 pieces will yield forty bite-sized hors d'oeuvres.

❖ *Roll-ups & Stacks* ❖

*Pictured clockwise from upper left: Tuna Roll-ups, Bologna Triangles, Ham Squares, Pickle Roll-ups, Asparagus Roll-ups & Salmon Spread Roll-ups.*

## Bologna Roll-ups & Stacks

8 slices cold cuts: bologna, ham or turkey
8-ounce tub of favorite spreadable cream cheese,
    plain or flavored with herbs

**For roll-ups**: Spread cream cheese filling evenly over 4 slices of bologna. (Use remaining 4 slices to make bologna stacks below.) Roll up tightly and wrap in plastic wrap. Refrigerate several hours or overnight until firm. To serve, trim uneven ends from each side of roll-up, cut crosswise into 3 or 4 bite-sized pieces and arrange on a tray. Yields 12 to 16 cut roll-ups.

**For stacks**: Using the 4 remaining bologna slices, begin by spreading cream cheese filling evenly over one slice. Make a second layer by covering with another slice spread with additional filling. Repeat with a third slice spread with cream cheese filling and top with fourth slice. Wrap the stacked slices in plastic wrap and refrigerate several hours or overnight until firm. To serve, cut into triangles or squares and arrange on a tray. Yields about 18 bologna squares or triangles, depending on size.

❖ *Finger Food for Parties* ❖

## Salmon and Cucumber Cream Cheese Stacks

5 slices firm white sandwich bread
8-ounce tub salmon cream cheese
6.5-ounce tub cucumber dill
    cream cheese

*More Roll-ups*

Trim crusts from bread slices. To flatten bread slices, moisten a clean tea towel and lay it across a chopping board. Place two slices of bread on upper half of towel. Fold the remaining half of the towel over the slices. With a rolling pin, roll to flatten the bread slices. Spread the first slice with the salmon cream cheese. Make a second layer by placing another flattened bread slice over the first. Spread this second slice with the cucumber dill cream cheese.

Moisten and flatten the three remaining bread slices. Continue the layers by adding the third flattened bread slice spread with the salmon cheese spread and then the fourth flattened bread slice spread with the cucumber spread. Top with the fifth flattened bread slice. (There will be cream cheese leftover.) Wrap with plastic wrap and refrigerate for several hours or overnight. To serve, slice into squares and arrange on a tray. Makes about 9 to 12 hors d'oeuvres depending on the size of the cut squares.

## Ham Squares With Cheddar & Capers

¼ to ½-inch thick slice of ham
Cheddar slices for topping
Capers, for topping

Preheat oven to 350 degrees. Place ham on a cutting board and top with a single layer of thin cheddar slices. Cut into squares and arrange on a baking sheet. Heat in the oven for about five minutes until the cheese melts slightly but doesn't bubble. Remove from oven, pressing a caper into cheese while it is soft. To serve, arrange on a tray. Yields about 9 squares depending on size of cut hors d'oeuvres.

## Pickle Roll-ups

6 slices firm white sandwich bread
6 medium-sized sweet gherkin pickles
8-ounce tub favorite cream cheese spread

Trim crusts from bread slices. To flatten bread slices, moisten a clean tea towel and lay it across a chopping board. Place two slices of bread on upper half of towel. Fold the remaining half of the towel over the slices. With a rolling pin, roll to flatten the bread slices. Peel away the towel from the flattened bread slices and spread with the cream cheese.

Place a pickle on top of the cream cheese at one end of the flattened bread slice. Roll up tightly. Repeat the process with the remaining bread slices, cream cheese and pickles.

Wrap the pickle roll-ups in plastic wrap and refrigerate for several hours or overnight.

To serve, trim the uneven ends of the roll-ups and slice crosswise into 3 or 4 bite-sized pieces. Arrange the cut roll-ups attractively on a tray. Yields about 18 to 24 cut hors d'oeuvres.

## Asparagus & Ham Roll-ups

6 asparagus spears
Dijon mustard
6 slices ham
6 slices mozzarella cheese

Blanche asparagus by heating in a pan of boiling water for 5 minutes; drain and cool. Spread mustard on ham slices and top with cheese slices. Place an asparagus spear at one end; roll up tightly. Arrange on a baking pan and heat in a 350-degree oven for 6-8 minutes. Cut each roll-up into 5 pieces and arrange on a tray. Yields 30 hors d'oeuvres.

## SALAMI & WATERCRESS HORS D'OEUVRES

*Wrap thinly-sliced salami slices around a few sprigs of washed and dried watercress. Secure with a party toothpick. Arrange on a tray.*

NEW BABY · NEW COUNTRY

*C*ooking in Germany was a new challenge. *I arrived on July 3, 1969, with a three-month old baby propped on my hip. As Gene was enjoying his first moments with his newborn son, I was acclimating myself to unfamiliar surroundings and to a kitchen with a refrigerator the size of a postage stamp. The U.S. Army had decided this would be our home for eighteen months and I was going to make the best of it. I was soon roaming the open-air markets under the shadows of medieval cathedrals and experiencing the richness of a new country and cuisine.*

❖ *Hunter Style Chicken* ❖

## HUNTER STYLE CHICKEN

1 frying chicken, cut into serving pieces
Salt and pepper to taste
2 tablespoons olive oil
2 tablespoons butter
2 ounces brandy
8-ounce package fresh mushrooms,
    washed, dried and sliced
$\frac{1}{4}$ cup chopped scallions
4 tablespoons chicken broth
$\frac{1}{4}$ teaspoon dried rosemary
$\frac{1}{4}$ teaspoon dried thyme

Rinse chicken under running water and pat dry with paper towels. Remove skin, if you'd like less fat, and season with salt and pepper. In a frying pan, brown chicken well in oil and butter. Pour the brandy over browned chicken and ignite with a match. Transfer chicken to a warm platter.

Saute mushrooms and scallions in the frying pan, adding four tablespoons of chicken broth to scrape up the browned bits of chicken that are stuck to the bottom of the pan. Add herbs and sauté a few more minutes. Pour mushrooms and scallions over the chicken and serve with German Potato Salad (recipe follows). Serves 4-6.

### German Potato Salad

2 pounds potatoes, peeled and cut into cubes
4 slices bacon
2 tablespoons olive oil
4 scallions, chopped
2 tablespoons red wine vinegar
1 tablespoon capers
1 teaspoon salt
$\frac{1}{2}$ cup mayonnaise
$\frac{1}{2}$ cup ripe pitted olives
2 hard boiled eggs, shelled and sliced

Drop cubed potatoes into boiling, salted water and cook until tender, about ten minutes. Remove from heat, drain and set aside.

Sauté bacon until crisp; blot on paper towels and set aside. Pour off bacon drippings and add two tablespoons of oil to the pan. Sauté chopped scallions about two minutes; add vinegar, capers and salt. Pour over potatoes and toss. Stir in mayonnaise, garnish with olives, egg slices and crumbled bacon. Serves 4 to 6 as a side dish.

## ❖ *Potato Soup* ❖

3 medium red potatoes

½ cup sliced carrots

1 tablespoon butter or margarine

Salt and pepper, to taste

3 tablespoons light olive oil

4 tablespoons flour

½ cup chopped onion, precooked with
 some water in microwave to soften

1 can (14.5 ounces) diced tomatoes

1 tablespoon sugar

8-10 fresh mushrooms, washed and sliced

Optional: ½ cup frozen green peas or
 shelled soybeans (Edamame)

Optional: 2 (5-inch) links sweet Italian
 sausage, pork or turkey, cooked
 and sliced

POTATO SOUP:

Wash and cube potatoes, leaving skins on for more fiber. Cook potatoes and sliced carrots in 4 cups of salted water for 10 minutes. Drain vegetables reserving three cups of cooking liquid. Toss the cooked potatoes and carrots with butter or margarine; salt and pepper to taste.

In a heavy Dutch oven pan, heat oil over medium heat and add flour, stirring constantly until light brown. This will take about 10 minutes depending on heat setting. The mixture, called a roux, should be brown in color, but don't let it burn! Remove from burner; add one cup reserved cooking liquid and stir vigorously with a wire whip to remove any lumps.

Return to stovetop and stir in precooked onion with another cup of reserved cooking liquid to make a smooth gravy. Add canned tomatoes and sugar; stir.

Add cooked potatoes and carrots with enough of the remaining cooking liquid to make a nice thick soup.

Add mushrooms and cook for about 10 minutes more. If using peas, soybeans and/or sausage, add with mushrooms during last 10 minutes of cooking. Thin the soup with additional cooking liquid if needed. Serve with a salad and a loaf of crusty bread. Total cooking time is about 35 to 40 minutes. Serves 4.

*My first trip to the local grocer was a quick study on shopping customs in Germany. After bringing several items to the check-out counter and promptly paying for them, I waited for the items to be bagged. Nothing happened. I looked at the cashier looking at me and waited. She waited. Seconds ticked by and I began to sweat. When she realized that I had not brought along my own bag, which was the custom, she reached for some paper sacks from the nearby bakery section and bagged my purchases. I struggled home balancing a baby on one hip and a couple of grocery-filled sacks on the other. Never again. On the next outing, I made sure I carried my own leather shopping bag with me.*

*Carrying Jim in my German shopping bag.*

❖ *Wiener Schnitzel* ❖

## WIENER SCHNITZEL

*Wiener Schnitzel (breaded veal cutlet) was our favorite take-out meal in Germany. Gene would pick up schnitzels mit pommes frites (French fries) at a local restaurant whenever we wanted a quick meal. It's quite easy to make, but in this version the cutlets are sauteed in olive or canola oil instead of deep-fried and served with buttered white asparagus (spargel) instead of French fries.*

1 pound veal cutlets, cut $\frac{1}{2}$ inch thick
Salt and pepper to taste
1 beaten egg
Breadcrumbs
4 tablespoons olive or canola oil
Lemon slices
Optional: capers, for garnish

Cut the veal cutlets into 2 or 3 serving pieces and season with salt and pepper. Dip in egg, then coat with breadcrumbs.

Heat oil in a frying pan over medium-high heat and sauté cutlets on both sides until golden brown. This will only take about ten minutes.

Transfer the cutlets to a warm serving dish and garnish with the lemon slices and capers. Serves 2.

*Dining out with a baby requires some tricky manuevers. Gene or I would often have to take turns eating our meal inside while the other paced outside with our fussing son. Take-out food was a better choice and, in Germany, Wiener Schnitzel was our favorite.*

## SAUERBRATEN

2 ½ to 3 pounds London Broil
2 cups wine vinegar
2 cups water
1½ teaspoons salt
1 teaspoon ground black pepper
2 tablespoons dried parsley
3 whole cloves
1 bay leaf
2 tablespoons sugar
1 onion, sliced

1 tablespoon flour, for dusting meat
3 tablespoons olive oil
2 tablespoons tomato puree
4 tablespoons cold water
2 tablespoons flour
1 cup beef stock
6 gingersnaps, broken into crumbs

Place meat in a deep glass dish. Mix vinegar, water, salt, pepper, parsley, cloves, bay leaf, sugar and onion slices. Pour over meat, cover and refrigerate for 2 days turning daily.

Remove meat from the refrigerator. Drain marinade and reserve. Pat meat dry with paper towels and lightly dust with one tablespoon of flour. Brown in heated oil over medium-high heat in a heavy Dutch oven pan. Add tomato puree and three cups of reserved marinade, including onion slices, to meat. (Discard any unused mari-

nade.) Cover and simmer about two hours until meat is tender. Transfer meat to a warm platter. Remove bay leaf from the marinade. Mix the four tablespoons of cold water with the two tablespoons of flour and stir into the hot marinade. Add stock and gingersnap crumbs and continue to cook over medium-high heat until marinade thickens into a gravy, stirring occasionally. This will take about fifteen minutes. Serve gravy with meat. Yields 6 servings. Serve with Red Cabbage.

### Red Cabbage

1 head red cabbage
1 teaspoon wine vinegar
2 tablespoons olive oil
1 tablespoon chopped onion
2 tablespoon sugar
2 tablespoons wine vinegar
1 tablespoon red wine

Wash cabbage, blot with paper towels and shred. Add one teaspoon of wine vinegar to a pot of boiling salted water. Add the shredded cabbage and cook, covered, for five minutes or until tender. Drain and set aside. Heat oil in a saucepan and sauté the onion until soft; stir in boiled cabbage. Mix sugar, two tablespoons of wine vinegar and red wine; pour over cabbage. Cook, covered, for 15 to 20 minutes. Serves 4 as a side dish.

❖ *Sauerbraten* ❖

*1969, Lampertheim, Germany*

*M*any wonderful pastry shops were within walking distance of our apartment in Lampertheim. Strudels with fruit fillings were among our favorites.

# APPLE STRUDEL

*U*se phyllo dough measuring 8 ¹/₂ x 12 ¹/₂ inches. There are usually two packs in a box and you can find it in the freezer section of most grocery stores. It takes about two hours to thaw the phyllo sheets, an hour and a half to prepare and another 40 minutes to bake the strudel. It's a bit time-consuming but it's well worth the effort.

¹/₂ box (one 8-oz. pack) phyllo pastry sheets
¹/₄ cup golden raisins
White wine

1 pound tart green apples
1 tablespoon fresh lemon juice
¹/₂ cup granulated sugar
¹/₄ cup coarsely chopped walnuts
³/₄ teaspoon cinnamon
¹/₂ cup (1 stick) unsalted butter, melted
1 cup finely ground walnuts
Confectioners sugar, for dusting

Thaw phyllo pastry sheets according to package directions. Plump raisins by cooking in wine to cover, for about 15 or 20 minutes. Set aside to cool.

Peel, core and thinly slice the apples; sprinkle with lemon juice. Mix the granulated sugar, the chopped walnuts and the cinnamon. Toss with apples and mix in the cooled, plumped raisins.

Preheat oven to 375 degrees. Dampen a tea towel, place on a flat surface and cover with waxed paper. Open the thawed phyllo pastry sheets and place on top of the waxed paper. Fold the phyllo sheets over in half, like a book. The fold will be on the left. Begin opening the "book" by turning the first phyllo sheet or "page" to the left.

Using a pastry brush, paint the phyllo sheet with melted butter then sprinkle lightly with some finely ground walnuts. Continue to open the "pages" of phyllo sheets, painting each sheet with butter and sprinkling with ground walnuts until the "book" is open to the center. Fold the right side of the "book" over in half. This time the fold will be on the right. Open the first right-hand "page" or phyllo sheet, paint with melted butter and sprinkle with ground walnuts. Continue until all the "pages" or sheets are buttered and dusted with walnuts. Back at the center of the "book",

spread the apple-raisin filling along one of the longer edges of the dough and roll up, jelly roll fashion. Tuck in the ends and place, seam side down, on an ungreased baking sheet. A baking sheet with sides works best.

Brush with additional melted butter and bake for 30 to 40 minutes or until golden brown. Dust with confectioners sugar, slice crosswise and serve. Makes 8 to 10 slices.

❖ *Apple Strudel* ❖

*"Hmmm good!"*          *Winter, 1970*

*Getting a toddler to eat* proved to be an even more daunting task than cooking in a foreign country. After our return to the states in 1970, much of my time was spent cajoling, tricking or bribing our son Jim to eat. The daily tug-of-war at mealtime required lots of patience, cunning and creativity.

*"Not good!"*

Putting a "happy face" on a pancake, topping entrees with tomato sauce or ketchup became a part of meal preparation. The daily dance at dinnertime resulted in many funny stories and lots of innovative food prep in the kitchen. Breakfast foods and desserts emerged as our toddler's favorites; recipes in this section reflect his preferences.

❖ *Smiley Face Pancakes* ❖

# SMILEY FACE PANCAKES

1 cup buttermilk baking mix
1 egg, lightly beaten
½ cup cold water

⅓ cup sour cream
Topping: pure maple syrup
Optional: butter, for serving

Beat baking mix, egg, water and sour cream with a spoon until smooth. If you mix the batter in a large 4-cup glass measuring cup, it will be easier to pour it onto the griddle.

Preheat griddle, and when it is hot, pour about half a cup of batter onto the griddle pan to make a large 5-inch pancake. Make the "eyes" and "mouth" by forming a funnel out of waxed paper. Pour a little batter into the funnel, snip off the tip and squeeze batter slowly onto griddle to form two dots for "eyes" and a crescent-shaped line for the "smile".

When bubbles appear on the pancake, flip it over to cook on other side. Carefully lift the "eyes" and "mouth" and position on pancake to form a smiley face. The uncooked sides of the "eyes" and "mouth" will adhere to the top of the cooked side of the pancake. Repeat until all batter is used. Makes three 5-inch smiley face pancakes, enough for one toddler and mommy too. Serve with syrup and butter.

Note: To make a larger quantity of pancakes, increase baking mix to 2 cups and use one egg, ¾ cup of cold water and ⅔ cup of sour cream.

**"Frowning Face Pancakes"**: If your toddler wakes up as an unhappy camper, simply invert the smile to form a pouting mouth. It will surely bring a smile albeit a reluctant one.

## ❖ *Orange French Toast* ❖

1 large orange
3 eggs, beaten
4 tablespoons unsalted butter
6 slices firm white bread
½ cup orange marmalade
Confectioners sugar, for sprinkling
Cooked bacon slices, optional

Grate orange peel to remove zest (outer orange rind) and set aside. Squeeze the juice from the orange reserving two tablespoons. Add rest of orange juice and grated zest to the eggs and mix well with a fork.

Melt unsalted butter in skillet. Dip bread slices in egg mixture and brown on both sides. Remove from pan, cut each slice in half to form triangles and arrange on a warm platter. Repeat with rest of bread slices.

Mix the two tablespoons of reserved orange juice with marmalade and heat in microwave for 30 seconds or until warm. Spoon over French toast, sprinkle with confectioners sugar and serve with crisp slices of bacon. Makes six slices (twelve triangles).

## Oven-baked Pancake

½ cup all-purpose flour
½ cup whole milk
2 eggs, lightly beaten
⅛ teaspoon nutmeg
4 tablespoons (one-half stick) unsalted butter
Confectioners sugar, for sprinkling
Assorted jams and jellies

Preheat oven to 425 degrees. Combine flour, milk, eggs and nutmeg in a bowl and beat lightly leaving batter a little lumpy. Melt butter in a 10-inch oven-proof skillet . When skillet is very hot, pour in batter and bake in oven for 15 minutes or until golden brown. Sprinkle with confectioners sugar and serve with assorted jams and jellies. Serves 4.

*Reading a bedtime story. Sept., 1970*

### What's for Breakfast?

*After each night's bedtime story, Jim would ask me what I was making for breakfast the next morning. He fell asleep with dreams of piping-hot waffles swimming in syrup or pancakes smiling up from his plate.*

❖ *Oven-baked Pancake* ❖

### ❖ *Zucchini Pancakes* ❖

## ZUCCHINI PANCAKES

*In order to prove to Jim that there were other vegetables besides potatoes, corn and green beans, I substituted zucchini for the potatoes in the potato pancake recipe that he liked. As I predicted he ate the zucchini pancakes without a word. Feeling victorious I asked him how he enjoyed the zucchini. He jumped back from his plate and cried, "Where?" "They were in the pancakes", I replied smugly. From that day forward Jim wouldn't eat potato pancakes for fear I would sneak in some other vile vegetable that he refused to eat.*

3 cups chopped zucchini
2 tablespoons milk
2 eggs
1 small onion, quartered
3 tablespoons flour
1 teaspoon salt
$\frac{1}{4}$ teaspoon baking powder
4 tablespoons unsalted butter, for frying

If the zucchini are small, there's no need to peel them, unless you are trying to sneak them into the recipe. In that case, peel them so the green tint won't give them away. If the zucchini are large and have a tougher peel, remove it.

Place chopped zucchini in a food processor or blender. Add milk, eggs, onion, flour, salt and baking powder; pulse until blended but still a little chunky. Preheat a griddle or skillet to medium-high heat. When it is hot, melt a tablespoon of unsalted butter on the surface and pour zucchini mixture onto pan in $3\frac{1}{2}$-inch sized pancakes. When golden brown, carefully flip to brown other side. The surface of the griddle needs to be hot enough to make a crisp pancake, but not too hot so as to brown too quickly. The pancake needs to cook about five to eight minutes on each side for it to be cooked thoroughly inside. If the pancakes are too thick add another tablespoon of milk; if the pancake batter is too thin and doesn't hold together as it is flipped, add a tablespoon of flour.

Melt additional unsalted butter in the griddle to fry the rest of the pancakes. Makes one dozen $3\frac{1}{2}$-inch zucchini pancakes.

*"How did you like the zucchini, Jim?"*
*"Where?" "They're in the pancakes!"*

# LASAGNA

*Italian food had always been popular in the Bratek family, and it quickly became a favorite food for Jim as well. Pasta and tomato sauce was easy to eat as a toddler (see the photograph on page 41) and it sustained him through his teenage years. Today lasagna remains one of his favorite meals.*

**Tomato Sauce:**

2 (5-inch) links sweet Italian sausage,
    pork or turkey
1 pound ground round
3 tablespoons olive oil
1 small onion, chopped
1 clove garlic, minced
1 can (1 lb. 12 oz.) tomato puree
1 can (6 oz.) tomato paste
1 teaspoon dried oregano
1 tablespoon dried parsley
1 bay leaf
$\frac{1}{4}$ teaspoon pepper
$\frac{1}{2}$ teaspoon salt
1 tablespoon sugar

1 box (1 lb.) lasagna noodles
1 container (15 oz.) ricotta cheese
1 pound (16 oz.) mozzarella cheese, grated
Grated Parmesan cheese, for sprinkling

To make sauce: Place sausage links on a paper towel-lined pie plate and microwave on high for three minutes, stopping half way through to turn pieces over. Set aside to cool before cutting into thin slices.

Crumble ground round into hot skillet and brown thoroughly. Remove from heat, drain off fat and set meat aside.

In a deep Dutch Oven pan, heat olive oil and sauté chopped onion until translucent. Add minced garlic on top of onions but do not brown. Stir in tomato puree with $\frac{3}{4}$ can of water, the tomato paste with 3 of the small cans of water, and the seasonings. Add the thin slices of cooked sausage and the browned meat and simmer, uncovered, for $1\frac{1}{2}$ hours.

Bring a large pot of salted water to a boil and add lasagna noodles. Cook for half the recommended time or about 5 to 6 minutes. Drain and blot on paper towels.

To assemble the lasagna: Preheat oven to 350 degrees. In an oblong baking dish (13"x 9"x 2"), spread a few tablespoons of tomato sauce over the bottom of the pan. Lay three cooked lasagna noodles over the tomato sauce. Spread with some ricotta cheese, sprinkle with some mozzarella cheese and add another thin layer of tomato sauce. Repeat layering of lasagna noodles, ricotta and mozzarella cheeses and tomato sauce for a total of five or six layers, topping the last layer with the remaining ricotta and mozzarella cheeses, some of the tomato sauce and a sprinkling of Parmesan cheese. Bake in the oven for 35 to 40 minutes or until the cheeses are melted and sauce is bubbling. If the sauce starts bubbling over the side of the lasagna pan while baking, line a cookie sheet with aluminum foil and place on bottom rack of the oven to catch the sauce. When done, remove the lasagna pan from the oven and let it stand for about 15 or 20 minutes before cutting into twelve equal squares. Serves 12.

Note: Serve any leftover tomato sauce on the side.

❖ *Lasagna* ❖

❖ *Chocolate Train Cake* ❖

# CHOCOLATE TRAIN CAKE

*As Jim's third birthday approached, a photograph of a Circus Train Cake appeared in a magazine. Jim's love of trains was well established by this time; the cake was perfect for his upcoming birthday party. The "recipe" involved using a prepared cake mix and frosting mix. That was the easy part. Cutting the cake pieces, frosting and decorating was a bit time-consuming. However, seeing Jim's happy response (see photo below) made it worth the extra time. A favorite homemade chocolate cake and frosting could be used instead of the prepared mixes, if desired.*

1 package chocolate cake mix (for 2-layer
    cake)
1 package chocolate fudge frosting mix
    (for 2-layer cake)
Animal crackers, mini-marshmallows
Assorted candies: Gum drops, cinnamon
    candies, chocolates, peppermints,
    licorice, etc.

Prepare chocolate cake according to the package directions. Grease a 13 x 9 x 2-inch baking pan or line it with parchment paper. Pour batter into pan and bake according to package directions. Remove from pan; cool.

Cut the sheet cake into eight pieces, about 4x3-inches each. Seven of these cake pieces, standing upright on the long side, are the "train cars". The eighth piece will be used to fashion the odd pieces needed to make the extra parts of the engine and the rounded tops of some of the other cars.

Frost each "train car" cake piece and decorate with the assorted candies and cookies. Serves about 16.

Note: I made a three-car train and simply cut the rest of the sheet cake in squares, frosted them and topped them with candies. As long as the pieces of chocolate cake have frosting and candies on top, the kids at the birthday party will eat them!

*Jim's Third Birthday*         *March 15, 1972*

## Chocolate Cheese Mini-Cupcakes

**Filling:**

8-ounce package cream cheese

Dash salt

$\frac{1}{3}$ cup sugar

1 egg

6-oz. package semi-sweet chocolate chips

**Cake:**

2 $\frac{1}{4}$ cups all-purpose flour

$\frac{1}{3}$ cup +2 tablespoons baker's cocoa

1 $\frac{1}{2}$ teaspoon baking soda

$\frac{3}{4}$ teaspoon salt

1 $\frac{1}{2}$ cups sugar

$\frac{3}{4}$ cup vegetable or canola oil

$\frac{1}{2}$ tablespoon white vinegar

1 $\frac{1}{2}$ cups cold water

1 $\frac{1}{2}$ teaspoon vanilla extract

For filling: Beat cream cheese, dash of salt, sugar and egg in an electric mixer until smooth: stir in chocolate chips. Set aside.

For cake: Preheat oven to 350 degrees. In a large bowl sift flour with cocoa, baking soda and salt. In bowl of electric mixer, beat the sugar, oil and vinegar until mixed. Add sifted flour mixture alternately with the 1 $\frac{1}{2}$ cups of cold water, beginning and ending with the flour mixture. Add vanilla extract and beat briefly.

To assemble: Line mini-cupcake pans with mini-cupcake papers and pour the batter until half full. Spoon about a teaspoon of the chocolate chip/cream cheese filling on top of batter. Bake in oven for 15 minutes.

Remove from oven and let cool in pans for ten minutes. Place in air-tight containers and refrigerate until ready to serve. These little cupcakes freeze well. Simply remove from freezer and allow to reach room temperature and serve. Makes between 6 or 7 dozen mini-cupcakes.

❖ *Chocolate Cheese Mini-Cupcakes* ❖

## Mini-Cream Puffs

### Filling:

3-oz. package vanilla pudding and pie mix
1 ½ cups milk
½ cup heavy cream
2 tablespoons confectioners sugar
½ teaspoon vanilla

### Cream Puffs:

½ cup water
4 tablespoons (one-half stick) butter
⅛ teaspoon salt
½ cup all-purpose flour
2 large eggs

For filling: Cook pudding according to the package directions, using only 1 ½ cups of milk. Pour into bowl and place waxed paper directly on surface of pudding. Refrigerate for one hour.

Beat heavy cream, confectioners sugar and vanilla just until stiff. Remove pudding from refrigerator and fold into whipped cream mixture. Cover and refrigerate.

For cream puffs: Preheat oven to 400 degrees. In a saucepan, combine water, butter and salt and bring to a boil over medium heat. Remove from heat; add flour all at once and beat with a wooden spoon until mixture leaves sides of pan and forms a ball, about one or two minutes. Add eggs, one at a time, beating well after each addition; dough will be satiny. Drop by level teaspoons, two inches apart, on an ungreased cookie sheet. Bake 20 to 25 minutes until golden brown. Let cool before slicing and filling with custard. Serve immediately. Makes 36.

❖ *Mini-Cream Puffs* ❖

# GINGERBREAD COOKIES

*Every Christmas when Jim was young, I would bake gingerbread cookies, wrap them in plastic wrap and attach them to presents or hang as ornaments on the tree. The wonderful scent of cinnamon and ginger filled our kitchen and signaled that another holiday season had begun.*

**Cookies:**

1 cup (2 sticks) unsalted butter
1 cup firmly packed light brown sugar
½ teaspoon grated lemon rind
3 teaspoons grated orange rind
2 teaspoons ground cinnamon
1 tablespoon ground ginger
1 cup molasses
2 eggs, lightly beaten
6 cups sifted all-purpose flour
½ teaspoon salt
1¼ teaspoon baking soda

**Icing:**

2 egg whites
Pinch of salt
3 to 3½ cups confectioners sugar
1 teaspoon fresh lemon juice
Raisins, for "eyes" and "buttons"

Trace the patterns for the 8-inch gingerbread boy and girl on pages 174 and 175.

Cream butter with sugar until light and fluffy. Mix in grated rind and spices. Bring molasses to a boil; stir into butter mixture until thoroughly blended. Beat in eggs. Mix flour, salt and baking soda; add to mixture gradually, beating until dough forms a ball. Wrap in wax paper; refrigerate for one hour.

Preheat oven to 350 degrees. Divide dough into 6 pieces; roll out one piece on a lightly floured surface to about the size of your gingerbread pattern. Line cookie sheet with parchment paper and place the rolled out dough on top. Lay pattern on top of the dough tracing around it with a knife; remove excess dough as you cut. Press raisins into dough for "eyes" and "buttons". Repeat with rest of dough, gathering the scraps of dough together to make more cookies. Bake for 15 minutes. Remove from oven, cool on racks. When cool, decorate with icing (directions follow). Makes twelve 8-inch cookies.

To make icing: Beat egg whites, salt, 3 cups of confectioners sugar and lemon juice with an electric mixer until stiff peaks form. Add more sugar if needed to make a stiff paste. Fill a pastry bag with some of the icing and pipe an outline along outer edge of cookie and add a "smile".

❖ *Gingerbread Cookies* ❖

❖ *Painted Cookies* ❖

# PAINTED COOKIES

*Making personalized cookies for the family is great fun. I made soccer ball cookies for Jim, basketball cookies for Gene, and even transferred favorite photos onto cookies for special occasions (see below). Cut out pictures from magazines or coloring books. Make tracings of family photos. Buy some small paint brushes and have fun.*

2 cups all-purpose flour
2 cups cake flour
1 teaspoon baking powder
$\frac{1}{2}$ teaspoon salt
1 cup (2 sticks) unsalted butter
$1\frac{1}{2}$ cups sugar
2 large eggs
2 teaspoons pure vanilla extract
1 teaspoon lemon extract

**"Paint":**
5 egg yolks
2 teaspoons water
Food coloring

Preheat oven to 350 degrees. Sift all-purpose flour, cake flour, baking powder and salt in a large bowl. Set aside.

Cream butter with sugar until light and fluffy. Beat in eggs and extracts. Stir in flour mixture gradually to make a stiff dough.

*May 1972*

Roll out a portion of the dough on top of a sheet of parchment paper. Lay the tracing of the picture on top of the dough and with a large pin point, prick holes along outlines. Remove tracing and with a knife, cut along the outer shapes, gathering up scraps of dough as you cut. Reuse scraps to make more cookies.

For "paint": Mix yolks and water; divide among 5 cups. Add a few drops of food coloring to each cup to make red, yellow, blue and green. In the fifth cup, add drops of red, blue and green to make black. With a new, small paint brush, paint outlines with black and fill with other colors. Lift painted cookies with parchment sheet. Place on cookie sheet; bake in oven for 15 minutes. Cool on racks. Continue with rest of dough. Makes about a dozen cookies depending on size.

*Fall 1973*

MY · MOMS · AND · ME

　　　　　　　　　　　　　　　　　　　　　　　　　　　　　*Fall, 1984*

*A*s my cooking skills improved, *honed in part from the experience of cooking in Germany and of trying to satisfy a finicky eater, it seemed a good time to face the challenge of recreating family recipes. With my mother Helen's help and my mother-in-law Corrie's guidance, I expected little trouble. How naive a daughter/in-law*

*can be! After many unsuccessful attempts with their sketchy recipes, I decided on a new strategy. I watched them prepare their masterpieces and took copious notes. It was interesting to see how many steps were left out of their recipes. But the three of us had fun in the kitchen chatting, chopping and laughing our way through the recipes. A sampling appears in this section.*

*Charlotte, NC*                    *December, 2003*

❖ *Pierogies* ❖

*Mom Millus* *is Polish and potatoes have been featured prominently in her daily meal planning. That was perfectly fine with my father who was a meat-and-potatoes person. Mashed potatoes, skillet fries, potato pancakes and potato-filled pierogies were all very popular at our house. When I started to cook in the first weeks of marriage, it never occurred to me not to include potatoes with our evening meal. After about a month, Gene asked if we could please have something other than potatoes. I was puzzled, "Like what?" I asked. "Well, maybe rice or noodles", he suggested. "What a concept," I thought as a newlywed in 1966.*

## PIEROGIES

**Dough:**

3 cups all-purpose flour

Pinch of salt

$\frac{1}{2}$ cup plus 2 tablespoons warm water

1 large egg

I tablespoon sour cream

**Potato and Cheese Filling:**

4 cups (about 5 medium) potatoes, peeled
   and cubed

8 ounces (2 cups) shredded cheddar cheese

**Toppings:**

Melted butter

Chopped onions, sautéed in butter

To make dough by hand: Sift flour and salt into a large bowl; make a well in the flour. In a separate bowl, beat warm water, egg and sour cream; pour into bowl with flour. Work flour into liquids with your fingers until dough no longer sticks to your fingers or to the sides of the bowl. Add more water if the dough is too dry and crumbly or more flour if too sticky. Knead dough about five minutes. Cover and let it rest for 15 minutes.

To make dough in food processor: In the bowl of processor, pulse flour and salt on and off a couple of times. In a small bowl, beat warm water, egg and sour cream.

Gradually pour liquids into processor pulsing on and off until dough leaves sides of bowl and forms a ball. On a floured surface, knead dough for five minutes. Cover and let it rest for 15 minutes.

Roll out dough on a floured board to $\frac{1}{16}$ of an inch thick. Use edge of a glass or cup to cut 3-inch rounds. Fill each dough round with one rounded tablespoon of filling (directions follow) and fold in half. Pinch edges together well to seal; let rest 5 minutes.

Cook filled pierogies, about 4 or 5 at a time, in boiling salted water until they rise to the surface, about 2 minutes. Cook four minutes longer; remove with slotted spoon; drain in colander. Keep warm in covered dish while cooking rest of pierogies. Serve with melted butter and sautéed onions. Yields: 2 dozen.

To make Potato/Cheese Filling: In a saucepan, bring potatoes to a boil in salted water. Cook for 20 minutes until soft. Drain and mash. Add cheddar cheese and mix thoroughly. Use as filling for pierogies.

*October, 1999*

## STUFFED CABBAGE

*"Piggies", as we called them, can be made with ground beef or turkey. My mom always used tomato soup diluted with water for her sauce, while my mother-in-law used tomato sauce. It tastes delicious either way.*

1 large head of green cabbage
2 cups cooked rice
1 small onion, chopped
1 pound ground beef or turkey

Salt and pepper to taste
1 egg or equivalent egg substitute
2 cans (10 ¾ oz. each) tomato
   soup

Wash cabbage, discarding any wilted outer leaves, and remove core. Add to a large pot with water to cover. Bring water to a boil; reduce heat and cook until leaves are tender but not too soft. Remove outer leaves as they cook until ten leaves have been separated from the head; drain in a colander. Remove the rest of the cabbage head and use as a side dish for another meal. (I chop and sauté it in olive oil with bits of ham or bacon.)

Cook chopped onion in a little water in the microwave on high for two minutes until the onion is just tender; drain. In a large bowl, mix cooked rice with ground meat, cooked onion, salt and pepper and egg.

To assemble: Preheat oven to 350 degrees. Slice away part of the thick vein from each cabbage leaf, without cutting through the leaf. Divide filling mixture among the ten cooked cabbage leaves and roll up, tucking in sides as you roll. In a shallow baking dish, line up stuffed cabbage rolls, seam side down, in a neat row. Mix tomato soup with water according to directions on cans and pour over the cabbage rolls in the baking dish. Cover loosely with aluminum foil and bake in oven for 45 minutes until meat is cooked inside. Makes 10 stuffed cabbage rolls.

❖ *Stuffed Cabbage* ❖

*Pictured below: Walnut Bread and Prune and Nut Crescent Cookies*

❖ *Holiday Pastries* ❖

## HOLIDAY PASTRIES

*The Walnut Bread and Crescent Cookie recipes have been passed around our family through the generations. They usually are prepared during the holidays, but would be delicious any time of year. The walnut bread is moist and just sweet enough and the cookies are buttery and soft and very addictive.*

### Walnut Bread

**Sweet Bread Dough:**

4-5 cups all-purpose flour

3 tablespoons sugar

$\frac{1}{2}$ teaspoon salt

1 cup (2 sticks) butter, softened at room temperature

1 package dry yeast

1 cup milk, lukewarm

3 egg yolks

**Walnut Filling:**

$1\frac{1}{2}$ pounds walnuts, finely chopped in blender or food processor

$1\frac{1}{2}$ cups sugar

$\frac{1}{2}$ to $\frac{3}{4}$ cup hot milk, enough to moisten filling and keep nuts together

**Topping:**

2 tablespoons melted butter

By hand: In a large bowl mix 4 cups of flour, sugar and salt; add butter by pieces and mix with fingers until the mixture resembles coarse cornmeal. Dissolve yeast in lukewarm milk and stir gently; add yolks and mix. Make a well in the flour mixture and pour in liquid mixture. Slowly work the flour and liquids together with your fingers to form a dough, adding additional flour if dough is sticky. Knead on floured surface for 5 to 10 minutes. Return dough to bowl, cover and let it stand $1\frac{1}{2}$ to 2 hours or until double in bulk.

In Food Processor: With steel blade, pulse 4 cups of flour, sugar and salt until mixed; add softened butter by pieces and pulse on and off until the mixture resembles coarse cornmeal. Dissolve yeast in lukewarm milk and stir gently; add yolks and mix. Add liquids to bowl of processor, pulsing it on and off, until it forms a ball and leaves sides of food processor.

*Continued on page 66.*

*Walnut Bread - Continued from page 65.*

Add additional flour if the dough is too sticky. Remove dough from processor, place on floured surface and knead for about five minutes. Place in a deep bowl, cover and let rise 1¹⁄₂ to 2 hours or until double in bulk.

After Dough Has Doubled in Bulk: Preheat oven to 350 degrees. Divide dough into three parts. Roll out one part on a lightly floured surface forming a rectangle 10"x 13" and about ¹⁄₁₆ inch thick.

Spread one-third of the Walnut Filling (recipe follows) evenly over dough, then roll up jellyroll fashion and place on a greased cookie sheet. Repeat the process with the other two parts of dough. Let loaves rise 30 minutes before baking. Bake in oven for 40 to 45 minutes or until golden brown. Remove from oven; brush with melted butter; cool on racks. Cut into slices and serve. Makes 3 loaves.

To Make Walnut Filling: Mix walnuts with sugar and enough hot milk to moisten.

## Prune and Nut Crescent Cookies

**Dough:**
8 ounces (1 cup) margarine, softened
8 ounces cream cheese, softened
2 ¹⁄₂ cups all-purpose flour
Confectioners sugar, for rolling out dough

**Prune Filling:**
20 pitted prunes
1 tablespoon sugar

**Walnut Filling:**
¹⁄₂ pound walnuts, ground finely
¹⁄₂ cup sugar
1 tablespoon butter, softened
Hot milk, enough to moisten mixture

Preheat oven to 350 degrees. In an electric mixer, beat the margarine and cream cheese until creamy. Remove bowl from mixer; stir in flour gradually with a wooden spoon; knead into a dough. Roll out part of the dough on a surface dusted with confectioners sugar. Cut into 2-inch squares; fill with a teaspoon of Prune or Walnut Filling (directions follow). Fold two opposite corners of dough over filling, bend slightly into a crescent shape and arrange on a greased cookie sheet. Repeat process with rest of dough. Bake in oven for 15 to 20 minutes. Makes about 5 to 6 dozen cookies.

To make Prune Filling: Place pitted prunes in a saucepan and cover with water. Cook until prunes are soft. Drain excess water and mash prunes with the sugar.

To make Walnut Filling: Mix all ingredients in the order listed above.

# ❖ *Fresh Pumpkin Pie* ❖

*Once you've tried a pumpkin pie made from a fresh pumpkin, you will never go back to using the canned version. My mother has always made it this way; it's a little more work to cut up the pumpkin (get your family in on the fun!) but it's worth it.*

3 cups fresh pumpkin filling (see directions below)

2 eggs, slightly beaten

¾ cup sugar, half brown and half granulated

2 tablespoons pumpkin pie spice

1 can (12 oz.) evaporated milk

9-inch unbaked pie crust

Optional: whipped cream, for garnishing

To cook fresh pumpkin: Cut pumpkin in half; remove seeds and stringy part. Cut pumpkin into 1-inch strips, then 1-inch square pieces. Remove rind from pieces and place in a large pot with enough water to cover. Bring to a boil and cook until soft, about 45 minutes. Drain in a colander, mashing pieces well to remove excess liquid. Continue to drain in colander and push out liquid. Reserve 3 cups of mashed pumpkin to make one pie. Freeze any remaining pumpkin, in 3-cup portions, for later use.

To make pumpkin pie: Preheat oven to 425 degrees. Mix 3 cups pumpkin with eggs, sugar, spice and milk. Pour into unbaked pie shell. Bake 15 minutes; lower oven temperature to 350 degrees and continue baking 35-40 minutes or until a knife inserted near center comes out clean. Cool, cut into wedges and add a dollop of whipped cream to serve. 6-8 servings.

❖ *Peach and Pineapple Squares* ❖

## PEACH & PINEAPPLE SQUARES

*These tasty fruit squares are so moist and delicious and can be made with any kind of canned fruit. The recipe has been made in my family for generations, always with the peach and pineapple fillings. My mom and my Aunt Lil (pictured below) took turns making them for all of our family get-togethers.*

**Peach and Pineapple Filling:**
2 cups sugar, divided
6 tablespoons cornstarch, divided
2 cans (20 oz. each) crushed pineapple
2 cans (29 oz. each) sliced peaches

**Dough:**
4 to 5 cups sifted all-purpose flour
1/4 teaspoon salt
1 cup margarine
2 eggs, lightly beaten
1 cup sugar
1 teaspoon baking soda
1 cup sour cream
1/4 cup milk, for rubbing on pastry
Confectioners sugar, for dusting

To make Fillings: Mix one cup sugar and 3 tablespoons cornstarch with the undrained pineapple in top of a double boiler. Cook until thickened; pour into a bowl and set aside to cool. Cook undrained peaches with other cup of sugar and three tablespoons of cornstarch. Cook until thickened and cool.

To make the Dough: Mix four cups of the flour with the salt in a large mixing bowl. Work margarine into flour with fingertips until mixture resembles coarse cornmeal. Combine beaten eggs, sugar, baking soda and sour cream. Add to flour mixture and mix to form a dough, adding the additional cup of flour as needed to make a smooth dough.

Divide dough into 3 portions. Roll out one portion and fit it into one of two baking sheets (each 10 1/2" x 15 1/4"). Repeat with second portion, leaving the third portion to make lattice tops.

To assemble: Preheat oven to 350 degrees. Roll out remaining dough and cut into lattice strips 1/2 inch wide. Spread peach filling onto dough in one baking sheet; spread pineapple filling on the other baking sheet. Top with lattice strips and dot with a little milk. Bake in oven for about 20 minutes. When pastry is cool, cut into squares. Arrange them on a serving platter and dust with confectioners sugar. Makes 3 or 4 dozen, depending on size of squares.

*Mom and Aunt Lil    October, 1996*

Manville, NJ                    Summer, 1981

**Mom Bratek** *was born and raised in the South. Growing up in the farm region of western North Carolina rooted her to the soil and solidified her love of the outdoors and gardening. Her backyard gardens overflowed with a variety of vegetables - the bigger the better. At harvest time, vegetables were brought directly from the garden to the stove, cooked simply and enjoyed. My earliest memory of sitting down at her table, was the sight of so many fresh vegetables. There simply was not enough room on our plates for all that she had prepared. What she didn't prepare fresh, she canned for the winter or shared with family and friends.*

❖ *Garden Vegetables* ❖

## GARDEN VEGETABLES

*Mom Bratek seldom used written recipes for cooking fresh vegetables. Her meals were down-home delicious with lots of vegetables served family-style at the table. She would watch her guests carefully to ensure that no vegetable was overlooked. "Did you see the beans?" would be her polite way of reminding you that you missed a helping of beans even though your plate was overflowing.*

### Southern-style Green Beans

1 pound green beans, trimmed and cut
    into bite-sized pieces
1 slice bacon, chopped, or 1 tablespoon
    canola oil
Salt and pepper, to taste
1 tablespoon butter

Cook beans with chopped bacon or oil and just enough water to cover. Bring to a boil; reduce heat and simmer, covered, for 30 minutes until tender. Drain and toss with butter. Serves 4.

### Fried Okra

1 tablespoons flour
1 tablespoon cornmeal
Salt and pepper, to taste
1 pound okra, cut into ¼-inch slices
3 tablespoons canola oil, for frying

Combine flour, cornmeal, salt and pepper; toss with sliced okra to coat lightly. Heat oil in a heavy saucepan large enough for okra to be in one layer; fry okra over medium heat until golden brown. Serves 4.

### Southern Fried Squash

See recipe on page 18.

### Three Bean Salad

*Freshly cooked vegetables can be used in this recipe, but canned vegetables are much easier.*

1 can (14.5oz.) cut green beans
1 can (14.5oz.) cut yellow beans
1 can (14.5oz.) red kidney beans
¼ cup diced red pepper
¼ cup diced green pepper
¼ cup diced onion
½ cup sugar
½ cup white wine vinegar
½ cup canola oil

Drain the beans; add diced peppers and onions. Mix sugar and vinegar; heat in microwave for 30 minutes and stir until sugar is dissolved. Add to beans with oil and toss. Serves 4-6.

*Savannah, GA Summer, 1984*

# RATATOUILLE

3 tablespoons olive oil
1 large onion, thinly sliced
1 clove garlic, minced
3 zucchini, thinly sliced
1 yellow squash, thinly sliced
1 red bell pepper, seeded and cut into
    pieces
1 eggplant, cut into 1" cubes
3 medium tomatoes, diced, or 1 can
    (14.5 oz.) diced tomatoes with juice
1 teaspoon salt
1 teaspoon dried basil
1 teaspoon dried parsley
1 tablespoon sugar
Grated Parmesan cheese, for sprinkling

In a large frying pan heat the olive oil and sauté the sliced onion until limp. Add garlic, zucchini, yellow squash and red pepper and sauté for about 10 minutes.

Mix in the eggplant, tomatoes, salt, basil, parsley and sugar and cook slowly for about 30 minutes. Serve sprinkled with Parmesan cheese. Makes about 8 servings.

Note: Ratatouille may be served as a light luncheon meal or as a side dish; it's great with lamb chops and mashed potatoes. As a main meal, cook a couple of sweet Italian sausages; slice and add to the ratatouille. Serve hot over freshly cooked pasta and serve with a nice loaf of crusty bread spread with butter.

*Bridgewater, NJ*          *Summer, 1981*

*G**ene shared his mother Corrie's love of gardening** and her competitive streak. While Mom Bratek strived to outshine her son with the ripest tomatoes and the largest zucchini, Gene challenged her by experimenting with a wide variety of vegetables and fruits such as soybeans, new strains of cantalope, and fraises des bois (wild strawberries) which he planted in a pyramid on our deck in New Jersey (see the photograph above).*

*Gene also planted a "ratatouille" garden, growing all the ingredients needed to make the vegetable medley: onions, peppers, zucchini, eggplant and tomatoes. The recipe appears on this page and is pictured on the opposite page.*

❖ *Ratatouille* ❖

## ❖ *Meatloaf* ❖

1 small onion, chopped
1 1/2 pounds ground meat (combination of
    ground beef, veal and pork)
6-8 slices bread
Warm milk, for soaking bread
1 egg
1 tablespoon dried parsley
Salt and pepper, to taste
2 tablespoons barbecue sauce, for topping

**Gravy:**
1 cup plus 3 tablespoons canned beef
    stock, divided
1 tablespoon cornstarch

Preheat the oven to 400 degrees. Place the chopped onion in a deep bowl with a couple of tablespoons of water; microwave on high for about 2 to 2 1/2 minutes. Drain and add the ground meat. Dip the bread slices in warm milk, squeezing out excess milk. Add bread to the bowl with the meat and the onions. Mix in egg, parsley, salt and pepper and form into a log shape. Place in an oiled roasting pan and top with barbecue sauce. Place in the oven, reduce heat to 350 degrees and roast for about an hour. Let meatloaf sit for 10 minutes; transfer from roasting pan to a serving platter and cover with foil to keep warm. Makes 10-12 slices.

To make gravy: Heat roasting pan on stove top; add one cup of beef stock scraping up browned bits on bottom of pan. When liquid starts to bubble, combine cornstarch with 3 tablespoons of beef stock and add to pan stirring until gravy becomes thick and smooth. Pour through a sieve and serve.

Meatloaf is great with mashed potatoes, green beans and cole slaw. Leftover meatloaf slices make delicious sandwiches.

# ❖ *Almond Coffee Ring* ❖

*Cakes were Mom Bratek's specialty - coffee cakes, layer cakes, sheet cakes; she whipped them up with ease. This coffee cake is great for breakfast, brunch or even a bake sale.*

1 package dry yeast
⅓ cup milk
⅔ cup granulated sugar
3½ to 4 cups all-purpose flour
3 large eggs, lightly beaten
½ cup canola oil
¾ teaspoon salt
1 can (12½ ounces) almond filling

**Icing:**
1 cup confectioners sugar
1 tablespoon warm milk
Additional milk to make a smooth
   paste

**Garnishes:**
Maraschino cherries, cut in half
Walnut halves

    In a large bowl dissolve yeast in lukewarm milk (95-110 degrees); allow to stand for five minutes. Add sugar and one cup of flour, stirring well with a wooden spoon.

*Continued on page 76.*

*Almond Coffee Ring continued from page 75.*

Combine eggs, oil and salt and stir into bowl. Gradually add rest of flour until dough is no longer sticky and can be formed into a ball. Turn out on counter and knead, adding additional flour if needed. Place in a deep, lightly oiled bowl, cover with a dampened dish towel and let rise in a warm place until double in bulk, about 2 hours.

Punch down dough and knead on counter for about a minute or so, working in more flour if needed. Roll out to an oblong shape about ¼ inch thick. Spread with almond filling and roll up jellyroll fashion. Shape into a circle on a round baking sheet and join the ends. Cut slits at several places around the outside of the ring, stopping about an inch from the center to keep the ring intact. Turn the slices at the slits to expose some of the filling. Let rise again for about 30 minutes.

Preheat oven to 350 degrees; bake for 30 minutes. Reduce oven to 325 degrees if it starts to brown too quickly. Cool completely.

For Icing: Beat confectioners sugar and enough warm milk to make a smooth paste. Drizzle over cooled coffeecake and garnish with cherries and walnut halves. Cut into 8-10 slices and serve. To freeze: Wrap slices in plastic wrap and foil. Defrost later and serve.

## POUND CAKE

*M*om Bratek liked to experiment with recipes, but sometimes the end product did not turn out well. In this pound cake recipe, she tried adjusting the amount of eggs and baking time, but each attempt resulted in an undercooked cake and it fell or it was overcooked and dry. She persisted and finally got it right. When I inherited her recipes, I found many variations for the same recipe. There were three distinctly different recipes (one is pictured on the opposite page) for her pound cake. After much experimenting on my own, I finally got it right too!

1 cup (2 sticks) butter, softened to room temperature
½ cup vegetable shortening
3 cups sugar
Pinch salt
5 eggs, room temperature
3 cups cake flour
½ teaspoon baking powder
1 cup whole milk
1 teaspoon vanilla extract
½ teaspoon lemon extract
Confectioners sugar, for dusting

Preheat oven to 350 degrees. Grease and flour a 10-inch tube pan.

*Continued on page 77.*

*Pound Cake continued from page 76.*

*Mom Bratek's Original Recipe*

Beat butter and shortening in an electric mixer on high speed until mixed well. Add sugar gradually and continue to beat until mixture is light and fluffy, about three minutes. Reduce mixer speed to medium and add eggs, one at a time, mixing well after each addition. In a separate bowl, combine flour and baking powder. At lowest speed of mixer alternately add the flour mixture (in fourths) and the milk (in thirds) beginning and ending with flour. Be sure to beat thoroughly after each addition. Blend in extracts and pour batter into prepared tube pan. Bake in oven for 1 hour and 10 minutes or until tester inserted near center comes out clean. Let cool upright for 10 minutes, then invert on a rack to cool completely. Dust the top of the cake with confectioners sugar. Makes 12 to 16 slices depending on thickness.

❖ *Pound Cake* ❖

❖ *Red Velvet Cake* ❖

# RED VELVET CAKE

1 cup (2 sticks) butter, softened

1 ½ cups granulated sugar

2 large eggs

2 teaspoons cocoa

2 ounces red food coloring (2 bottles)

1 teaspoon salt

1 teaspoon vanilla

1 cup buttermilk

2 ½ cups sifted cake flour

1 teaspoon baking soda

1 ½ teaspoons white vinegar

**Cream Cheese Icing:**

8 ounces cream cheese, softened

4 tablespoons (½ stick) unsalted butter, softened

1-pound box confectioners sugar

½ teaspoon vanilla extract

1 teaspoon cake flour (prevents frosting from sliding down the side of the cake)

*February 14, 2000*

*Gene's mom made a heart-shaped Red Velvet Cake each year for his Valentine's Day birthday. After Gene and I were married, his mom gave me the heart-shaped cake pans and I continued the delicious tradition.*

Have all ingredients at room temperature. Preheat oven to 350 degrees. Cream butter and sugar on high speed until fluffy, about 5 minutes. Reduce mixer to medium and add eggs, one at a time, beating well after each addition. Mix cocoa and food coloring until cocoa is dissolved and add to creamed mixture. In a separate bowl, combine salt, vanilla and buttermilk. Beating on low speed, alternately add the flour (in fourths) and the buttermilk mixture (in thirds), beginning and ending with the flour. Mix baking soda and vinegar and fold into mixture (don't beat). Divide cake batter evenly in two 9-inch or three 8-inch cake pans that have been greased, floured and lined with paper. Bake in oven for 30-35 minutes. Cool 10 minutes, then turn out onto racks to cool completely.

To make icing: Beat cream cheese with butter on high until smooth and creamy. On low speed stir in the confectioners sugar, vanilla and cake flour and beat until smooth. Spread between layers and on top and sides of cooled cake. Makes 10 or 12 slices.

HEADMASTER'S · WIFE

*H*osting parties in our new southern locale *was exciting but a little intimidating. Gene had just been named head of school at St.Andrews in Savannah and welcoming faculty and trustees to our home would be an important part of the job. Planning was crucial. I created an "entertainment book" in which each event was detailed: dates, guest lists, menus, etc. Sketches were added, a natural extension of my graphics work, to ensure an attractive presentation. The books have multiplied in number but remain an excellent record of events. A few book entries and recipes follow.*

❖ *Candy Cookies* ❖

# COOKIES & MILK PARTY

*Cookies are a favorite of both young and old, which make them ideal for an after-meal dessert for adults and an anytime treat for kids. Whether homemade or store-bought, cookies satisfy every sweet tooth. The trick is to arrange the cookies in a pretty basket lined with colorful tissue paper and sprinkle them with powdered sugar. Cookie baskets make wonderful centerpieces for sit-down luncheons or dinners. And for the little munchkins, decorating cookies with candies makes them irresistible!*

## Candy Cookies

$\frac{1}{2}$ cup (1 stick) unsalted butter, softened
$\frac{1}{2}$ cup shortening
1 cup light brown sugar, firmly packed
$\frac{1}{2}$ cup granulated sugar
2 large eggs
2 teaspoons vanilla extract
$2\frac{1}{4}$ cups all-purpose flour
1 teaspoon baking soda
1 teaspoon salt
$\frac{1}{2}$ cup chocolate coated raisins
Additional candies, for decorating tops
Confectioners sugar, for dusting

Preheat oven to 375 degrees. Cream butter and shortening until smooth; add sugars. Beat in eggs and vanilla. In a separate bowl, sift flour, baking soda and salt, and add gradually to creamed mixture, mixing well. Stir in one-half cup of chocolate coated raisins. Drop dough in 2-3 tablespoon portions , two inches apart, onto a parchment-lined cookie sheet. Press additional candies on top of dough and bake for 10-12 minutes. Cool and dust with confectioners sugar. Makes about $1\frac{1}{2}$ dozen $4\frac{1}{2}$-inch cookies.

*In order to become better acquainted with our students, Gene and I hosted a series of parties at our home. For the lower grades, we tried "cookies and milk", "make-your-own sundaes", and "hot dogs on the deck" parties, but no matter what we served the highlight of each gathering remained having the headmaster drive them over in the school van! For the older students, we hosted "deli sandwiches & soda" parties where Gene would entertain students' questions in a kind of "how am I doing" format. The food was kept simple, students enjoyed the time away from school and Gene and I appreciated spending time with our students.*

*Cookies & Milk Party    Fall, 1983*

# WINE & CHEESE PARTY

*A wine and cheese party is a relatively easy party to prepare. Invite some friends, offer a variety of cheeses and a nice selection of red and white wines and the fun begins! In the fall of 1983, Gene and I did just that and opened the doors of our home on Wilmington Island to our faculty and trustees along with their spouses for a wine and cheese party. I found some handy cheese markers in a kitchenware store in Savannah that helped identify the various cheeses for our guests. We offered an assortment of soft and hard cheeses as well as some cheese spreads, added crackers and fruit to the trays and served them at room temperature. I also baked a small round of Brie wrapped in a puff pastry sheet and it got rave reviews. Everyone loved the wonderful melted cheese that oozed out of the warm flaky crust. The recipe follows.*

## Brie en Croute

8-ounce round of Brie
1 package puff pastry sheets (found in the
    freezer section of the grocery store)
1 egg yolk, lightly beaten

Preheat oven to 375 degrees. Thaw one puff pastry sheet according to package directions. (There are two sheets in a package; store other sheet in freezer for another time.) Roll out pastry sheet on a floured surface to flatten folded seams. (1) Place the Brie on the lower right corner. (See photos below.) (2) Fold over opposite corner of pastry sheet and form around Brie. (3) Cut away excess dough. (4) Moisten edges slightly with water and seal together pressing the dough under the round of Brie to make a smooth finish. Use excess dough strips to decorate the top of the Brie with a flower or leaf design; brush the surface with the beaten egg yolk and place in the preheated oven. Reduce heat to 350 degrees and bake for 25 or 30 minutes until golden brown. Serves 6-8.

To make a larger Brie en Croute: Use a 14-ounce round of Brie and two sheets of puff pastry for top and bottom crust.

❖ *Brie en Croute* ❖

❖ *Rolled Flank Steak* ❖

## CHRISTMAS PARTY

$\mathcal{W}$ith the Christmas tree lights on and a fire in the fireplace, Gene and I welcomed our guests to a Faculty Christmas Party at our home. All of the preparation work was done - plates, flatware, glasses and linens were rented, card tables and chairs were set up throughout the main rooms and a dinner buffet was arranged on the dining room table. The menu included some crudités and blue cheese dip, stuffed flank steak, a spinach salad, and some warm crusty French bread. To add some fun to the evening, guests were asked to bring a grab-bag gift, "something to relieve stress or to help you relax". The guests unwrapped some very creative items: a baby pacifier, bubble bath, a joke book (laughter), golf balls, bingo game, a soft foot pillow to name a few. A good time was had by all.

### Rolled Flank Steak

1½ to 2 pounds flank steak
3 (5-inch) links sweet Italian sausage,
   pork or turkey
1 tablespoon light olive oil
½ cup diced sweet onion
½ cup diced red pepper
½ cup diced green pepper
1 clove garlic, minced
½ cup diced zucchini, unpeeled
½ cup chopped mushrooms
1 cup stuffing mix with herbs
1 egg, lightly beaten
2 tablespoons chopped parsley
Salt and pepper, to taste
Barbecue sauce

Ask the butcher to butterfly the steak, or make a slice lengthwise down the center of the steak being careful not to cut all the way through. With the knife at an angle, split the steak open, like a book. Place the butterflied flank steak between two sheets of waxed paper and pound flat with a wooden mallet.

*Continued on page 88.*

*"Guests were asked to bring a grab-bag gift, something to relieve stress or to help you relax."*

*Christmas Party, December, 1984*

## ❖ *Crudités and Blue Cheese Dip* ❖

*Rolled Flank Steak continued from page 87.*

Set butterflied steak aside.

Remove casings from the sausages and crumble into a heavy skillet coated with vegetable oil spray; cook over medium heat until no longer pink. Remove from pan, break into pieces and blot with paper towels.

In the same skillet, add one tablespoon of olive oil and sauté onion, peppers, garlic, zucchini and mushrooms for ten minutes.

Preheat oven to 350 degrees. In a large bowl, combine cooked sausage, vegetables, stuffing mix, egg, parsley, salt and pepper. Spread mixture evenly over flattened flank steak leaving a $1/4$-inch border on all sides. Roll lengthwise and secure with string or metal skewers. Place seam side down in a shallow roasting pan and bake for 30 minutes. Brush with barbecue sauce and continue baking for 15 minutes. Remove from oven and let sit covered with aluminum foil for about 15 minutes. Slice and keep warm on a platter. Serves 8.

## Crudités and Blue Cheese Dip

Assorted cut-up vegetables: carrots, celery, cucumbers, cherry tomatoes, peppers, etc.

**Dip:**
½ cup mayonnaise
½ cup sour cream
1 tablespoon lemon juice
1 tablespoon white vinegar
1 tablespoon onion powder
½ teaspoon garlic powder
2 tablespoons dried parsley flakes
Salt and pepper, to taste

Combine all the dip ingredients and chill. Arrange cut-up vegetables attractively on a platter and serve with dip.

## Spinach Salad

**Dressing:**
¼ cup balsamic vinegar
1 teaspoon sugar
¾ cup light olive oil
½ teaspoon salt
¼ teaspoon pepper
1 teaspoon dried basil
1 teaspoon dried parsley
1 clove garlic, peeled
2 green onions (scallions)

1 tablespoon butter
2 slices bread, crusts removed
Garlic powder
½ pound Canadian bacon, cut into 4
thick slices  *Continued on page 90.*

### ❖ Spinach Salad ❖

*Spinach Salad continued from page 89.*

1 tablespoon light olive oil
10-ounce package fresh spinach washed,
   dried and chilled
4 hard-boiled eggs, chopped
4 whole white mushrooms, sliced thinly
Salt and pepper, to taste

To make the dressing: Combine vinegar, sugar, ¾ cup oil, salt, pepper, basil and parsley and pour into a cruet. Add the garlic clove and 2 green onions, cutting them to fit inside the cruet. Shake to mix thoroughly.

To make croutons: Melt butter in a non-stick frying pan. Place bread slices in pan and coat both sides with melted butter. Toast to a golden brown over medium heat. Sprinkle with garlic powder and cut into cubes. Set aside.

Cut the Canadian bacon into cubes. Heat 1 tablespoon olive oil in a skillet; add bacon cubes and brown lightly. Set aside.

Tear spinach into bite-sized pieces and arrange on four salad plates. Spoon a tablespoon or two of dressing over each plate of  spinach. Divide the bacon cubes, chopped eggs and sliced mushrooms evenly among the four plates. Top with croutons. Serves 4.

# P.T.O. LUNCHEON

*To show our appreciation to parent volunteers, Gene and I hosted a luncheon for the P.T.O. officers. Since the luncheon began at noon, most of the food was prepared in advance. Earthenware plates were warmed in the oven, ready for the food to be arranged and served. The menu served on February 2, 1984, was a seafood strudel, buttered snow peas and a tomato rose garnish added for color.*

## Seafood Strudel

*It takes two hours for the phyllo sheets to thaw, 45 minutes to prepare the strudels and 40 to 45 minutes to bake. The good news is the strudel can be made a day ahead and kept refrigerated, then baked the day it is served. This recipe makes two strudels. Leftover strudel can be refrigerated and reheated in a 350-degree oven for 15 minutes.*

1 box (two 8-oz. packs) phyllo pastry sheets

**Cream Sauce:**
2 tablespoons (¼ stick) unsalted butter
2 tablespoons flour
½ teaspoon Dijon mustard
¾ cup milk, room temperature
¼ cup heavy cream
Salt and pepper, to taste

**Filling:**
½ pound tilapia or sole fillets

*Continued on page 92.*

❖ *Seafood Strudel* ❖

*Seafood Strudel continued from page 90.*

¼ cup water
¼ cup white wine
Salt and pepper to taste
8-ounce container lump crabmeat
½ pound small cooked & cleaned shrimp
½ cup grated Swiss cheese
¼ cup freshly chopped parsley
½ cup breadcrumbs
½ cup grated Parmesan cheese
¼ teaspoon dry mustard
1 cup (2 sticks) unsalted butter, melted

**Toppings:**
Additional melted butter
2 tablespoons freshly chopped parsley
Grated Parmesan cheese

Thaw phyllo pastry according to package directions. (This takes 2 hours if frozen.)

To make cream sauce: Melt 2 tablespoons of butter in a skillet over medium heat; stir in flour. Remove from heat and whisk in mustard and milk. Return to heat; cook until thickened. Stir in cream, season with salt and pepper; cover and refrigerate.

Place fish fillets in a dish. Add water and wine. Cover and microwave on high until fish is flaky, about two minutes; do not overcook. Drain and cool; flake fish into pieces.

In a large bowl combine cooked fish, crab, shrimp, grated Swiss cheese, and parsley; toss with reserved cream sauce. Cover and refrigerate until ready to use.

Preheat the oven to 375 degrees. Combine breadcrumbs, Parmesan cheese and dry mustard; set aside. Dampen a tea towel, place on a flat surface and cover with a sheet of waxed paper. Open one package of thawed phyllo sheets and place on top of waxed paper. Fold phyllo sheets over in half, like a book. The fold will be on the left. Begin opening "book" by turning the first phyllo sheet or "page" to the left. Using a pastry brush, paint the phyllo sheet with melted butter then sprinkle lightly with breadcrumb mixture. Repeat painting and sprinkling each sheet until back to center. Fold the right side over in half, repeat process until all sheets are buttered and dusted. At the center, spread half of the seafood filling along lower edge of longer side, tuck in ends and roll up, jelly-roll fashion. Repeat process with the remaining phyllo dough. Place the two strudels, seam side down, on a buttered cookie sheet and brush with melted butter; bake for 40 to 45 minutes, occasionally brushing with additional melted butter. Remove from oven, brush with butter and sprinkle with parsley and Parmesan cheese. Makes two strudels; each strudel yields 8 slices.

## BARBECUES & COOKOUTS

*Because of the warm southern climate, outdoor gatherings were very popular in Savannah. Oyster roasts, pig-pickins' (barbecues) and low country boils were held throughout the year. Despite a busy school schedule, Gene and I enjoyed having friends over for relaxing informal dinners. Two of our favorites were a grilled version of the low country boil and a finger-licking good dinner of ribs and rice. Have plenty of napkins handy for your guests!*

## Low Country Grill

4 (5-inch) links sweet Italian sausage,
 pork or turkey
1 dozen jumbo shrimp
1 cup white wine
1 tablespoon butter, cut into pieces
1 dozen small new potatoes
Seafood Cocktail Sauce (recipe follows)
Sides: corn, green beans and cole slaw

 Place sausages in a large saucepan with a cup of water. Bring to a boil, reduce heat, cover and simmer for five minutes turning the sausages over to parboil on both sides.

*Continued on page 94.*

### ❖ *Low Country Grill* ❖

*Low Country Grill continued from page 93.*

Remove from heat; drain on paper towels.

Wash shrimp and slit to remove vein. Place in a deep dish, press a piece of butter under each shell and pour white wine over them. Set aside.

Wash the potatoes; no need to peel. Drop into a pot of boiling water; cook for ten minutes. Drain and set aside.

Preheat grill according to manufacturer's directions. Spray sausages and potatoes with cooking spray and grill, covered, over medium heat until browned.

Remove shrimp from wine and place on the grill. Grill about five minutes; turn shrimp over and cook for another five minutes or until shrimp turn pink. Transfer to a warm serving platter and serve with seafood cocktail sauce, corn, green beans and cole slaw. Serves 4.

## Seafood cocktail sauce

$\frac{1}{2}$ cup ketchup
1 tablespoon prepared horseradish
1 tablespoon fresh lemon juice
$\frac{1}{2}$ teaspoon onion powder
1 teaspoon sugar
$\frac{1}{2}$ teaspoon Worcestershire sauce
3 or 4 drops Tabasco sauce

Mix ingredients thoroughly and refrigerate until ready to use. Serve with shrimp.

# RED RICE & RIBS

## Savannah Red Rice

3 tablespoons light olive oil
$\frac{1}{2}$ cup chopped onion
$\frac{1}{4}$ cup diced red pepper
$\frac{1}{2}$ cup Canadian bacon, chopped
2 cups long grain rice
$\frac{1}{2}$ teaspoon salt
1 can (28 oz.) whole peeled tomatoes
2 tablespoons sugar

Heat oil in a skillet and sauté the onion and pepper for a few minutes until tender. Add chopped Canadian bacon, rice and salt and stir until rice is coated with oil. Drain the juice from the tomatoes into a large glass measuring cup and add water to make 4 cups. Cut tomatoes into pieces and sprinkle with sugar. Stir tomato pieces and the 4 cups of juice into the skillet and bring to a boil. Turn heat down, cover and simmer for twenty minutes. Toss rice with a fork and serve. Makes 6 to 8 servings.

## Barbecued Spareribs

4 to 5 pounds meaty pork ribs, cut into
    2-rib portions
Favorite barbecue sauce

Preheat oven to 350 degrees. Parboil ribs by placing meaty-side down in one layer in a large saucepan. (This might have to be done in batches.) Add water to a half-inch depth and bring to a boil. Reduce heat, cover and simmer for five minutes. Remove from heat and place ribs in a shallow baking pan. Continue parboiling the rest of the ribs.

Bake ribs, uncovered, in preheated oven for 30 minutes. Brush with barbecue sauce and continue baking for 30 minutes more, basting 2 or 3 times with additional sauce. Cut into individual ribs and serve with Savannah Red Rice. Serves 6-8.

❖ *Savannah Red Rice & Ribs* ❖

## SIDE DISHES & DESSERT

*Three wonderful dishes that evoke memories of Savannah are baked Stuffed Vidalia Onions, Brunswick Stew and for dessert, Southern Trifle. We enjoyed these dishes at restaurants in Savannah and at friends' homes. My versions are gleaned from all these sources.*

❖ *Stuffed Vidalia Onions* ❖

## Stuffed Vidalia Onions

6 medium Vidalia onions
Butter or oil, for sautéing
3 (5-inch) links sweet Italian sausage, pork or turkey
½ cup soft bread crumbs
½ cup grated Parmesan cheese
2 tablespoons dried parsley
¼ teaspoon dried thyme
Salt and pepper to taste
½ to ¾ cup milk or cream
½ cup beef broth
½ cup dry white wine
Additional butter, for topping
Parmesan cheese, for sprinkling

Peel the onions, cut off top ¼ of each and scoop out centers to make cups, leaving a ¼-inch thick shell. Place the onion cups in a covered saucepan with one cup of water and bring to a boil. Reduce heat and simmer 5 minutes; turn onion cups over and simmer 5 minutes more. Drain and set aside.

Chop scooped-out onions (about 1 cup) and sauté in a little butter or oil until soft. Remove casings from sausage links and crumble into skillet

96

with onions. Cook until sausage is no longer pink, breaking up sausage into small pieces as it cooks.

Drain off fat, return to low heat and add the breadcrumbs, Parmesan, seasonings and enough milk or cream to moisten; simmer five minutes. Remove from heat.

Preheat oven to 350 degrees. Divide stuffing among the six onion cups and place in an oven-proof casserole dish. Pour beef broth and wine over stuffed onions, dot each with a pat of butter and sprinkle with Parmesan cheese.

Bake the stuffed onions for 45 minutes, basting two or three times during baking time with the wine/broth mixture.

Remove from oven and serve the stuffed onions with extra broth poured over them; add an additional pat of butter, if desired. Serves 6.

Makes a great side dish for a hearty meal or serve as a light lunch or dinner with a salad and crusty bread.

## Brunswick Stew

*The stew ingredients can be adjusted to your family's tastes. Include favorite vegetables, use just chicken if you'd prefer, or turn up the heat with additional pepper flakes. It's your choice. I like to prepare the first part of the recipe a day ahead in order to refrigerate the stock overnight. It makes removal of the fat a little easier.*

*Continued on page 98.*

❖ **Brunswick Stew** ❖

*Brunswick Stew continued from page 97.*

1 whole chicken
1 pound flank steak
1 pork tenderloin
2 quarts cold water
2 tablespoons salt
½ teaspoon whole black peppercorns
1 tablespoon red pepper flakes
1½ cups chopped onion
1½ cups cubed potatoes
1 cup green beans
1 cup peas
2 cups sliced okra
2 cups baby lima beans
2 cups kernel corn
2 cans (1 lb.12oz. size) whole peeled
   tomatoes
2 tablespoons sugar
½ stick butter

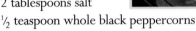

Put chicken, steak and pork tenderloin in a large soup kettle. Add water, salt, peppercorns and pepper flakes and bring to a boil. Reduce heat, cover and simmer for 2 hours or until meat is tender. Transfer chicken, steak and pork to a deep bowl removing bones, gristle and skin from chicken. Cover and refrigerate. Pour the stock into a deep, casserole dish. Cover and refrigerate several hours or overnight.

Remove solid fat from top of stock. Pour stock into a large kettle. Cut chicken, steak and pork into bite-sized pieces and add with the rest of the ingredients to the stock pot. Cook slowly, uncovered, for several hours. Serves 10 to 12.

## SOUTHERN TRIFLE

*This dessert can be layered in a large glass bowl (a trifle bowl would be pretty) or in individual dessert dishes. The pound cake and coconut macaroons can be homemade or store-bought; it's delicious either way. My version uses a raspberry sauce to douse the cake with instead of the traditional sherry.*

4.6-ounce package vanilla pudding and
   pie filling
3 cups milk
½ (10-ounce) package frozen raspberries,
   thawed
½ cup confectioners sugar
⅓ cup slivered almonds
Flaked coconut, for sprinkling
8 ounces (half pint) heavy cream
2 tablespoons confectioners sugar
4 (1-inch) wedges pound cake (store-
   bought or recipe, page 76)
4 coconut macaroon cookies (store-bought)
Assorted fruit: fresh strawberries, blueberries, raspberries, kiwis

In a saucepan, stir pudding mix into milk and cook over medium heat, stirring constantly, until mixture comes to a full boil.

Remove from heat and pour into a bowl; place plastic wrap right on surface of pudding and refrigerate until cool and firm.

Puree thawed raspberries with ½ cup of confectioners sugar in a processor. Press through a sieve to remove seeds; refrigerate.

Toast the slivered almonds and flaked coconut in preheated 350-degree oven for about five minutes, or until lightly browned.

Whip heavy cream with 2 tablespoons of the confectioners sugar until stiff. Refrigerate.

To assemble: Cut a cake wedge into cubes and place in a single layer on bottom of an individual glass dessert dish. Press slices of fruit against the side of the glass, anchoring in place with cake cubes. Spoon a tablespoon of the raspberry sauce over cake, crumble some coconut macaroon over the top, sprinkle with toasted almonds and add a thin layer of vanilla pudding. Continue to layer cake cubes, raspberry sauce, macaroon crumbles, toasted almonds and pudding as you line up the fruit along sides of the bowl. Repeat the process with other dessert dishes. Top with whipped cream; sprinkle with toasted coconut and serve. Serves 4-6, depending on the size of glass dessert dishes.

❖ *Southern Trifle* ❖

99

*M*oving to **Charlotte, North Carolina,** *and ultimately to a house on campus put our entertaining schedule in full swing. The house soon filled with Providence Day School faculty and staff, trustees and parents for*

*breakfast meetings, luncheons, receptions and dinners. The preparations for the different events included designing invitations, creating decorations for theme parties, and planning appropriate menus for each event. This section contains a highlight of events held at the headmaster's house and a sampling of the food served.*

# HEADMASTER'S DINNER

*Before moving into the headmaster's house, Gene and I hosted several events off campus. For Providence Day's annual auction we offered to prepare a special dinner for the winning bidders in their home. On September 26, 1987, eight invited guests were greeted with the aroma of freshly baked bread coming out of the oven. The diners were served appetizers by their headmaster, while in the kitchen the headmaster's wife (me) was adding the finishing touches to the Caesar salad, chicken Kiev and fresh vegetables. To top off the evening's meal, baklava was served warm with a dollop of vanilla ice cream on the side.*

## Homemade French Bread

1 package ($\frac{1}{4}$ ounce) dry yeast
4 tablespoons lukewarm water
1 cup cold water
2 tablespoons butter

3$\frac{1}{2}$ cups bread flour
1 teaspoon salt

**Glaze:**
1 egg, lightly beaten
$\frac{1}{4}$ teaspoon salt

In a small bowl, gently stir yeast into the four tablespoons of lukewarm water to dissolve. Let stand five minutes.

Heat the cup of cold water with the two tablespoons of butter over low heat until the butter melts. Remove from heat.

In a food processor, pulse the bread flour with the salt; add dissolved yeast and the water and melted butter. Blend for about 10 seconds until dough forms a ball. Place in a deep, oiled bowl, cover with a clean tea towel and let rise in a warm place for about an hour or until double in bulk.

Turn the risen dough out onto a lightly
*Continued on page 104.*

*September, 1987*

❖ *Homemade French Bread* ❖

*French bread continued from page 102.*

floured surface and knead for three to five minutes. Return to the bowl, cover and let rise for an hour or until double in bulk.

Preheat oven to 400 degrees. Turn dough out onto a lightly floured surface and press into a rectangular shape roughly 13 ½ inches by 9 inches. Roll up from the long side, jelly roll fashion and pinch seam together. Place seam side down with the ends tucked under into an oiled French bread pan or on a cookie sheet. Let rise in a warm place for about 30 minutes or until double in bulk.

Mix the lightly beaten egg with the ¼ teaspoon of salt and brush top of the bread. Bake in preheated oven for 30 minutes or until golden brown. Cool on a rack. Makes one loaf of French bread.

## Caesar Salad

4 quarts romaine lettuce, torn into bite-sized pieces

**Dressing:**
½ cup egg substitute
2 teaspoons Dijon mustard
3 tablespoons freshly squeezed lemon juice
⅓ cup light olive oil

❖ *Caesar Salad* ❖

# ❖ *Chicken Kiev* ❖

2 tablespoons grated Parmesan cheese
Additional Parmesan cheese, for sprinkling
Croutons

Beat egg substitute and mustard together with a wire whip. Slowly add lemon juice, beating constantly. Drizzle in olive oil while continuing to beat with the wire whip. Stir in two tablespoons of Parmesan cheese. Refrigerate until ready to use.

To serve, toss lettuce with dressing. Arrange on salad plates and sprinkle with additional Parmesan cheese. Top with croutons. Serves 8.

## Chicken Kiev

1 cup (2 sticks) butter, softened
$\frac{1}{4}$ cup finely chopped fresh parsley
2 cloves garlic, mashed
$\frac{1}{4}$ teaspoon cayenne pepper
2 tablespoons fresh lemon juice
2 teaspoons lemon zest
8 whole boneless chicken breasts
1 cup flour
4 eggs, lightly beaten
1 cup bread crumbs
Canola oil, for frying
Fresh parsley, for garnish

Mix softened butter with parsley, garlic

*Continued on page 106.*

*Chicken Kiev continued from page 105.*

and pepper. Beat in lemon juice and zest. Shape two tablespoons of the butter mixture into two cubes. (This will be used for pats of butter on top of each chicken roll when serving.) Form the remainder of the butter mixture into 8 elongated rolls, each about 2 ½ inches long. Wrap in aluminum foil and place in freezer for one hour.

Pound chicken breasts between sheets of plastic wrap until very thin. (You can ask the butcher to do this for you.) Cut off outer edges (use for chicken fingers another time) leaving a piece of chicken about 7 inches square. Remove elongated butter pieces from freezer and place one on each flattened chicken breast. Roll up and secure with toothpicks.

Preheat oven to 375 degrees. Dust each chicken roll well with flour, dip in beaten eggs and coat with bread crumbs.

Heat a cup of oil in a heavy saucepan and brown each breaded chicken roll on all sides until golden brown. Place in a baking dish and bake in oven for 12-15 minutes. Remove from oven and pull out toothpicks. Place on a serving platter garnished with fresh parsley. Cut the two reserved butter cubes into 8 pieces and place one piece on top of each breaded chicken roll. Serves 8.

❖ *Baklava* ❖

## BAKLAVA

½ box (one 8-oz. pack) phyllo pastry sheets
1 pound finely chopped walnuts
6 tablespoons sugar
1½ tablespoons cinnamon
½ cup bread crumbs
½ cup vanilla wafer crumbs
1½ cups (3 sticks) unsalted butter, melted

**Syrup:**
2 cups sugar
1 cup water
3 slices fresh orange
1 slice fresh lemon
1 cinnamon stick

Thaw phyllo pastry sheets according to package directions. Combine chopped walnuts, six tablespoons of sugar and cinnamon. Set aside. Mix bread crumbs and vanilla wafer crumbs in a small bowl and set aside.

Place thawed phyllo sheets on a sheet of waxed paper on top of a dampened tea towel. Cover with another sheet of waxed paper and another dampened tea towel. (This prevents the phyllo from drying out.)

Preheat the oven to 350 degrees. Brush melted butter over a baking sheet that has sides and is large enough to fit the phyllo sheets. Lay two phyllo sheets on the baking dish and brush the top sheet with melted butter. Sprinkle with cookie/bread crumb mixture. Repeat with two more layers, each layer having 2 phyllo sheets, brushing top sheet with butter and sprinkling with cookie/bread crumb mixture. Continue layering, but switch to the nut/sugar/cinnamon mixture until only six sheets of phyllo remain. Then switch back to sprinkling the layers with the cookie/bread crumb mixture for the final three layers. With a serrated knife, make six lengthwise cuts in the baklava, carefully holding down the top layers as you cut. Starting at one corner, make diagonal cuts across the baklava to create diamond shaped portions. Brush again with melted butter. Bake in oven for 40 to 45 minutes until pastry is nicely browned and crispy, basting every 10 minutes with additional butter. Cover with aluminum foil if top layer gets too brown.

Prepare syrup by combining all syrup ingredients in a saucepan and bringing them to a boil. Cook at a gentle boil for 20 minutes, stirring until the sugar is dissolved. Remove from heat and cool. Remove cinnamon stick and fruit slices; pour cooled syrup over hot baklava. Makes 2½ to 3 dozen pieces, depending on size.

## FACULTY LUNCHEONS

*A* *hurricane cancelled the first event scheduled at the headmaster's house for September 24, 1989. Hurricane Hugo swept through Charlotte downing trees and power lines. Five days later, without electricity, Gene and I welcomed alumni for a kick-off reception for Homecoming weekend. We improvised with lots of candles and take-out food from the few restaurants that were open, and we shared stories of hurricane damage and power outages.*

*Planning Sketch*

*Many social events have taken place at the house since that dramatic opening. The faculty luncheons were inaugurated in the fall of 1989. Each year Providence Day's teachers walked to the house for one of the three scheduled sittings and relaxed with their colleagues while a hot meal was served. The first menu was Chicken Pinwheels, cooked carrots, fresh rolls and Chocolate Cheese Mini-cupcakes (page 52) for dessert.*

*January 28, 1993*                                            *January 26, 1994*

❖ *Chicken Pinwheels* ❖

# CHICKEN PINWHEELS

4 whole boneless, skinless, chicken breasts

8 slices deli ham

**Filling:**

2 tablespoons butter

¾ cup grated sweet onion

½ cup grated Parmesan cheese

½ cup grated Gruyere cheese

2 cans (14 oz. each) artichoke hearts, drained and chopped

1 egg, lightly beaten

¼ cup freshly chopped parsley

1 tablespoon freshly chopped oregano

1-2 tablespoons olive oil

Herbs de Provence, available in specialty shops

Cut the chicken breasts in half; place between two sheets of plastic wrap and pound with a mallet until very thin. It may be necessary to butterfly thicker sections of the chicken breasts (slit part way through and open flat) in order to get them nice and flat. Place a slice of ham on each flattened chicken breast half.

For Filling: Melt butter in large skillet over medium heat and add grated onion. Saute 2 or 3 minutes then stir in grated cheeses and chopped artichoke hearts. Remove from heat and add egg, parsley and oregano.

Preheat oven to 350 degrees. Divide filling evenly into eight portions and form into

❖ *Spinach Lasagna* ❖

elongated rolls. Place one roll on top of each ham slice. Roll up, placing seam-side down, in a buttered baking dish, tucking ends under. Place them close together to keep from "unraveling". Brush with oil and sprinkle with Herbs de Provence (a mixture of rosemary, thyme, basil, savory, fennel and lavender). Bake, uncovered, in oven for 35 minutes. Cool or refrigerate for ease in slicing. To serve, slice cooled chicken breast rolls crosswise into pinwheels, thin for appetizers, thicker for an entrée. Pinwheel slices can be served hot or cold. To heat, arrange on an oven-proof platter; reheat in oven on low. Serves 8 as an entrée, 16 as an appetizer.

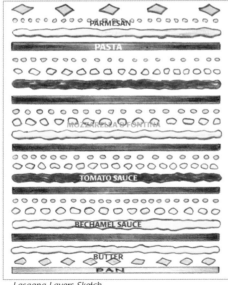

*Lasagna Layers Sketch*

# SPINACH LASAGNA

*After pounding 85 chicken breasts for the first luncheon with just one helper, I decided a new approach was needed. Two days before the second luncheon, a few PDS mothers gathered in my kitchen to help prepare Spinach Lasagna. The recipe included a red and a white sauce plus three different kinds of cheeses along with the green lasagna noodles. In order to avoid confusion in the order of layering, I drew a color coded sketch for us to follow. It definitely helped, but I got a lot of ribbing. "Doesn't everyone draw a sketch before they prepare lasagna!"*

**Tomato Sauce:**

2 tablespoons olive oil

³⁄₄ cup chopped onion

1 clove garlic, minced

1 can (6 oz.) tomato paste, mixed with
    4 cans water

1 teaspoon sugar

Salt and pepper, to taste

**Bechamel Sauce:**

¹⁄₄ cup butter or olive oil

¹⁄₄ cup flour

3 cups half and half, warmed in microwave

¹⁄₈ teaspoon white pepper

Pinch of grated nutmeg

¹⁄₄ cup grated Parmesan cheese

For assembly:

1¹⁄₂ boxes (1 lb. size) spinach lasagna
    noodles

*Continued on page 112.*

111

*Spinach Lasagna continued from page 111.*

8 ounces (about 1½ cups) grated mozzarella cheese

8 ounces grated Fontina cheese

¾ cup grated Parmesan cheese

½ stick butter, cut into pieces for top and
bottom of lasagna

To make tomato sauce: Heat 2 tablespoons of olive oil in a saucepan over low
heat and sauté onion and garlic for about ten
minutes. Stir in tomato paste and water; add
sugar, salt and pepper and simmer, uncovered, for 30 minutes.

To make béchamel sauce: Heat butter or
oil in saucepan; stir in flour until smooth.
Remove from heat and with a wire whip,
gradually add warm half and half, stirring
constantly to remove any lumps. Return to
heat and cook, stirring, over medium heat
until sauce is thick and smooth. Remove from
heat and stir in white pepper, nutmeg and
Parmesan cheese. Cover until ready to use.

Preheat the oven to 350 degrees. Cook
lasagna noodles according to package directions. Drain and set aside. Butter a 9 x 13-
inch baking pan, spread with one layer of
béchamel (white) sauce. Add a layer of
spinach (green) pasta and spread with
another layer of white sauce. Sprinkle with
some grated mozzarella and Fontina cheeses

and top with some Parmesan cheese. Add a
layer of green pasta then spread with a layer
of tomato (red) sauce. Sprinkle with the
three cheeses and repeat layering with
green pasta, white sauce and cheeses then
green pasta, red sauce and cheeses until the
final layer of green pasta, white sauce,
Parmesan cheese and pieces of butter. (See
color coded sketch on page 111.) Bake for
30 to 35 minutes or until lightly browned
on top. Cover and cool briefly before slicing. Makes 12 portions, 3 inches square.

# MUSHROOM & SAUSAGE FRITTATA

*A week before a faculty luncheon, I gave a cook-
ing demonstration for the volunteers who offered
to help prepare the frittatas. After preparing and
baking the dish, we all tasted a slice and dis-
cussed the logistics of bringing their baked frittatas to the headmaster's house the day of the
luncheon. It turned out to be a fun day and cer-
tainly made it easier for me. The menu included
the frittatas, Spinach Salad (page 89) and mini-
pecan tarts (from a local bakery). For centerpieces on all the tables, baskets were lined with
colorful napkins and filled with bread sticks and
a small pot of cheddar cheese spread. It looked
attractive and gave the teachers something to
nibble on until lunch was served.*

**Frittata:**

2 (5-inch) links sweet Italian sausage,
    pork or turkey

2 tablespoons olive oil

1 medium onion, chopped

8-ounce package mushrooms, washed and
    sliced

2 cups freshly chopped spinach

6 eggs

1 cup grated Parmesan cheese, divided

1 clove garlic, minced

½ teaspoon dried basil

¼ teaspoon dried marjoram

Salt and pepper, to taste

1 cup grated mozzarella cheese

*Cooking Demonstration*            *January 19, 1994*

Remove casings from sausages, crumble into a large non-stick skillet and brown over medium heat until no longer pink. Remove and drain on paper towels. Return skillet to heat; add the two tablespoons of oil. Sauté the chopped onion for about 5 minutes.

*Continued on page 114.*

❖ *Mushroom & Sausage Frittata* ❖

*Frittata continued from page 113.*

Add sliced mushrooms and cook for 5 minutes more. Remove from heat, drain liquid and set aside.

Preheat oven to 350 degrees. Butter a 9 or 10-inch pie plate. Layer the crumbled, cooked sausage evenly over bottom of pie plate. Then add a layer of the cooked onions and mushrooms and top with a layer of chopped spinach.

In a large bowl, combine the eggs, ¾ cup of the Parmesan cheese, garlic, basil, marjoram, salt and pepper and mix well. Pour egg mixture over spinach layer and top with the grated mozzarella cheese.

Sprinkle with the remaining ¼ cup of Parmesan and bake in the preheated oven for about 25 minutes or until the frittata is set and the top is golden brown.

Cool for about 10 minutes before cutting into slices. Serve with a fresh spinach salad (see recipe on page 89) and a crusty roll. Serves 6.

❖ *Manicotti* ❖

# MANICOTTI

*Panic struck the ranks of PDS volunteers when I suggested making Manicotti with homemade crepes for the faculty luncheon. "They're not so easy to make; not everyone cooks like you do." "Don't worry, I'll show you how to make them," I replied enthusiastically. Eight reluctant volunteers shuffled into my kitchen to watch the demo, skeptical that they would be able to recreate what they saw. With a non-stick 8-inch skillet in my hand, I poured in the batter, swirled it around and after a minute turned the crepe onto a plate. "Well sure, that looks easy when you do it." One by one, each volunteer tried her hand at making a crepe and was surprised how simple it really was.*

*Feeling confident that I had gained their trust, I suggested that we make cream puffs for dessert. After the uproar subsided and most scurried for the door, one of the women remained behind and volunteered...to order the cream puffs from a local bakery. "Don't push your luck" was the lesson I learned that day.*

**Tomato Sauce:**
Favorite recipe, or see page 48

**Pasta Crepes:**
1 cup all-purpose flour
1 cup water
1 large egg
$\frac{1}{2}$ teaspoon salt
Unsalted butter, for frying

**Filling:**
15-ounce container
 ricotta cheese
1 large egg
$\frac{1}{3}$ cup grated mozzarella cheese
1 tablespoon chopped parsley
Salt, to taste

Prepare the tomato sauce and while it is cooking, prepare the pasta crepes.

With a wire whip, beat flour, water, egg and salt until batter is smooth. Butter a non-stick, 8-inch skillet and heat over medium heat. Pour about $\frac{1}{4}$ cup of batter into the heated skillet, lifting pan slightly and swirling to spread the batter evenly. Cook for about one minute on one side only. Turn out of pan and continue cooking crepes until all batter is used. If the batter is too thick and does not spread well, add a teaspoon of water.

Preheat oven to 350 degrees. To make filling: Combine ricotta cheese, egg, mozzarella cheese, parsley and salt and mix thoroughly. Divide filling evenly among crepes, roll up and place, seam side down in a buttered baking dish. Top with some tomato sauce and bake in preheated oven for 25 minutes. Cover with aluminum foil if manicotti starts to dry out. Serve with extra tomato sauce. Makes 8 manicotti.

❖ *Seafood Paella* ❖

## TRUSTEE SOCIALS

*1997 Trustee Social*

*I*n 1989, the first Trustee event at the headmaster's house was a wine and cheese party similar to the one described on page 84. In 1991, a dinner format was established to take place after the final board meeting in the spring. It proved to be a perfect time to thank out-going board members and to welcome new trustees.

For the 1999 Trustee Social, a Mediterranean Buffet was served: a Seafood Paella, Ratatouille (page 72), Baked Fennel, Greek Salad, assorted olives and foccacia bread from a local bakery. For dessert: Grape Tarts and Baklava (page 106).

BAKED FENNEL

GREEK SALAD

RATATOUILLE

SEAFOOD PAELLA

FOCCACIA

## SEAFOOD PAELLA

1 (5-inch) link sweet Italian sausage,
   pork or turkey
1 whole boneless chicken breast
1 clove garlic
¼ cup olive oil
1 medium onion, thinly sliced
1 red pepper, chopped
1 cup uncooked rice (brown or white)
½ teaspoon salt
½ teaspoon saffron
2½ to 3 cups boiling water
1 can (6½ oz.) minced clams
1 cup snow peas (remove strings)
1 dozen Littleneck clams, washed to
   remove grit
½ to 1 lb. large shrimp, shelled and deveined

Place sausage on a paper towel-lined plate; cover with another paper towel and microwave on high for about 2 minutes. Turn sausage over and microwave on high for another 1½ to 2 minutes. Blot with paper towels, put in plastic bag and refrigerate for 1 hour. Grill chicken breast on both sides in a heavy skillet; put in plastic bag and refrigerate for 1 hour. Chilling allows for easier slicing.

To prepare paella: Remove sausage and chicken from refrigerator and cut into slices. Brown sausage slices in a skillet; set aside with chicken slices.

Heat garlic clove in olive oil in a heavy skillet until lightly browned; discard garlic. Add onion and red pepper to skillet and cook until soft. Add rice, salt and saffron; stir to coat rice with oil. Add 2½ cups of boiling water, minced clams and clam juice. Bring to a boil, lower heat to a constant simmer and cook uncovered for about 20 minutes (30 minutes if using brown rice). Add additional boiling water if needed. Add snow peas, reserved sausage and chicken slices and cook an additional 5 minutes. Place shrimp on top of paella, pushing down into rice. Cook until shrimp just turn pink. This will only take a minute or two.

Place clams on a rack with enough water to cover bottom of a deep pot. Cover and steam for 4 to 5 minutes, until shells open up. Discard any clams that do not open. Add steamed clams to paella. Keep warm until serving time. Serves 4.

## Baked Fennel

*Baked Fennel*

3 fennel bulbs
½ cup grated Parmesan cheese
½ cup bread crumbs
½ cup shelled pistachios, coarsely chopped
¼ cup golden raisins
½ teaspoon dried thyme
Salt and pepper, to taste
¼ cup olive oil

Preheat oven to 350 degrees. Cut off tops of fennel, wash bulbs and slice thinly.

Bring a saucepan of water to a boil and add fennel; simmer 5 minutes and drain. Arrange in one layer (slices will overlap) in an oiled baking dish.

Mix Parmesan, bread crumbs, pistachios, raisins, thyme, salt and pepper and toss with olive oil. Sprinkle evenly over fennel slices, pressing raisins into mixture to prevent them from burning. Bake in oven 20 minutes or until topping is golden brown. Serves 4.

## GREEK SALAD

**Vinaigrette Dressing:**

¼ cup white wine vinegar
¾ cup olive oil
1 tablespoon sugar
1 teaspoon dried oregano
Salt and pepper, to taste
1 green onion

1 head Romaine lettuce, cut into pieces
1 cucumber, sliced thinly
2 tomatoes, chopped
2 green onions, chopped
8 ounces crumbled Feta cheese
1 can (3.25 oz.) pitted black olives

Dried oregano, for sprinkling

To make dressing: Combine vinegar, oil, sugar, oregano, salt and pepper in a cruet and shake vigorously until thoroughly mixed. Add one green onion, cutting if necessary, to fit inside the cruet. Set aside.

To assemble the salad: Divide the lettuce among four plates. Arrange the cucumber slices, the chopped tomatoes and chopped green onions over the salads. Pour about two tablespoons of dressing over each salad and top with the crumbled Feta cheese and garnish with black olives and a sprinkling of oregano. Makes 4 side salads.

❖ *Greek Salad* ❖

## GRAPE TARTS

**Tart crust:**

2 cups all-purpose flour

$\frac{1}{8}$ teaspoon salt

$\frac{1}{4}$ cup sugar

$\frac{3}{4}$ cup (1 $\frac{1}{2}$ sticks) unsalted butter,
    cut into pieces

1 egg, lightly beaten

4 to 5 tablespoons ice water

**Cheese filling:**

8 ounces cream cheese, softened

$\frac{1}{4}$ cup sour cream

$\frac{1}{4}$ cup confectioners sugar

1 tablespoon Grand Marnier

**Glaze:**

$\frac{1}{4}$ cup light colored jelly or preserves
    (apple, peach, etc.)

$\frac{1}{2}$ teaspoon water

**Topping:**

Grapes: green, red and black seedless

To make tart crust: Place flour, salt and sugar in bowl of a food processor and pulse on and off a few times to mix. Add butter and continue to pulse until mixture resembles cornmeal. Slowly add the beaten egg and water while pulsing on and off until dough forms a ball. Turn out onto a floured surface and knead briefly until smooth. Chill dough while you prepare the filling.

To make filling: Beat cream cheese, sour cream and confectioners sugar until well mixed. Stir in Grand Marnier. Set aside.

To make glaze: If using preserves, put through a sieve to remove lumps. Add a little water if too thick. Set aside.

Wash grapes, blot on paper towels and cut in half crosswise to stand flat. Set aside.

Remove dough from refrigerator and let stand at room temperature for about 15 minutes. Preheat the oven to 375 degrees. Spray 12 round tart pans (3-inch diameter) with a non-stick vegetable spray.

Take a heaping tablespoon of tart dough and press it into tart pan with your fingers until it is spread evenly over pan. Repeat with rest of tart shells. Prick the bottom of each tart crust with a fork to prevent blistering during baking. Place tarts on a cookie sheet and bake in oven for 20 minutes or until slightly browned. Remove from oven and cool briefly before removing from pans.

Arrange the tart crusts on a tray and fill with 2 or 3 teaspoons of the cream cheese filling, leaving about $\frac{1}{4}$ inch of the crust exposed. Dip top of cut grapes into glaze and place, cut side down, on top of cheese filling. Or you can arrange the fruits first and then brush with glaze. Makes twelve 3-inch round tarts. Picture is on next page.

❖ *Grape Tarts* ❖

## Spring Buffet 2001

*The menu for the 2001 Trustee Social, held on May 16, included crab cakes, oven-roasted multi-colored potatoes, and a fresh spring salad.*

### Crab Cakes

2 (8 oz.) containers fresh lump crabmeat
2 tablespoons olive oil
½ cup finely chopped onion
½ cup finely chopped celery
½ cup bread crumbs
2 tablespoons dried parsley
Salt and pepper, to taste
2 large eggs, lightly beaten
1 tablespoon unsalted butter
1 tablespoon olive oil

Pick over crabmeat to remove hard cartilage and shell pieces. Set aside.

Heat two tablespoons of olive oil in a skillet and sauté the chopped onion and celery until soft. Remove from heat and add to crabmeat; stir in the breadcrumbs, dried parsley, salt, pepper and the beaten eggs.

Form into eight 3-inch patties. Melt butter with the one tablespoon of oil in a large skillet over medium heat. Add crab cakes and sauté until golden brown, about 5 to 8 minutes

*Invitation for Trustee Social*

per side. Makes 8 crab cakes. Serve with Oven-roasted Potatoes (recipe follows) and a fresh salad or spring vegetable.

### Oven-roasted Potatoes

*Use as many different colors and shapes of potatoes that you can find.*

2 dozen mini-potatoes in assorted colors
¼ cup olive oil
Salt and pepper, to taste

Preheat oven to 475 degrees. Wash and scrub potatoes and blot on paper towels. Cut larger potatoes into cubes. Pour a tablespoon or two of oil in a shallow roasting pan. Add potatoes in one layer; drizzle rest of oil over potatoes and toss. Season with salt and pepper. Roast in the preheated oven for 15-20 minutes, tossing potatoes occasionally to brown on all sides. Serves 6-8 as a side dish.

❖ *Crab Cakes & Oven-roasted Potatoes* ❖

# TRUSTEE SOCIAL 2003

*For the trustee social on May 14, 2003, many of the menu items were tried-and-true recipes that I have served over the years. In fact, the recipes for the baked apples and sweet potatoes can be found on page 13 in the "early years" section of this cookbook. I've been serving those recipes since the first year Gene and I were married. Pork tenderloins are also easy to make, always delicious, and will please a family of four or a crowd of fifty.*

*Invitation for Trustee Social*

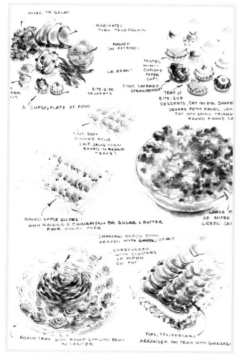

*Menu-Planning Sketch*

*Marinated Pork Tenderloin*

# PORK TENDERLOIN

1 package pork tenderloin (2 in a package)
Unseasoned meat tenderizer
1 can (8 oz.) pineapple slices, reserve juice

**Marinade:**
$\frac{1}{3}$ cup reserved pineapple juice
$\frac{1}{3}$ cup light soy sauce
$\frac{1}{3}$ cup olive oil
$\frac{1}{3}$ cup minced onion
1 clove garlic, minced
1 tablespoon brown sugar

Earlier in the day: Remove the two tenderloins from package and cut into 8 diagonal slices about $\frac{3}{4}$ inches thick. Place in a shallow glass baking dish large enough to hold slices in one layer. Moisten top of slices with water, sprinkle with tenderizer and prick the surface with a fork at $\frac{1}{2}$-inch intervals.

To make marinade: Measure ingredients in a glass measuring cup and stir to combine. Pour over pork slices, cover and refrigerate for 3 hours, turning slices half way through.

Preheat grill or broiler. Grill pork slices about 5 minutes per side. Brown pineapple slices for a minute on each side and serve with the pork. Serves 4-6.

## *Iceberg and Romaine Salad*

$\frac{1}{2}$ head Iceberg lettuce

1 head Romaine lettuce (large, flat, outer leaves removed)
$\frac{1}{2}$ cup peas, thawed if frozen
1 green onion, green part only, chopped
1 can (8 oz.) sliced water chestnuts, drained

**Dressing:**
1 cup mayonnaise
3-4 tablespoons milk
1 tablespoon sugar
Garlic powder, to taste
$\frac{1}{4}$ cup grated Parmesan cheese

**Garnishes:**
6 slices cooked crisp bacon, crumbled
3 hard-boiled eggs, shelled and chopped

Wash heads of lettuce at least one day before making the salad in order to crisp the lettuce leaves. Wrap in paper towels and store in a plastic bag in the refrigerator.

To make salad: Tear lettuce into bite-sized pieces and place in a large bowl. Toss with peas, onion and sliced water chestnuts.

To make dressing: Combine mayonnaise and milk until smooth. Spread over surface of salad and sprinkle with sugar, garlic powder and Parmesan cheese. Do not toss. Cover with plastic wrap and refrigerate.

To serve: Toss salad with dressing and garnish with crumbled bacon and chopped eggs. Serves 4.

❖ *Pork Tenderloin & Pineapples* ❖

# PINK & GREEN SOCIAL

*In 2005 the Trustee Social buffet was done in pink and green. The sketch below shows the table set with a pink tablecloth, pink and green napkins, and a green three-tiered centerpiece. Arranged on the centerpiece were pink petit fours and slices of Lime Meringue Pie (recipe follows). The main dishes included Chicken Breast Pinwheels stuffed with pink ham and green artichokes (recipe on page 110), Pasta Salad with green shells and pink ham (recipe follows), green kiwi wrapped in pink proscuitto, green snow peas and a pink and green shrimp-avocado salad.*

## Pasta Salad

16-ounce package any multi-colored pasta, cooked and drained
1 bunch fresh asparagus
4 ounces boiled ham, chopped
4 ounces mozzarella cheese, shredded
1 can (11 oz.) whole kernel corn, drained
1 jar (6 oz.) marinated artichoke hearts, quartered, undrained
1 can (3.8 oz.) pitted black olives
1/2 cup grated Parmesan cheese

**Dressing:**

1/2 cup mayonnaise
2 tablespoons milk
1 teaspoon Dijon mustard
2 tablespoons grated Parmesan cheese

*Menu-Planning Sketch*

128

Place the cooked pasta in a large bowl. Snap off tough ends of asparagus stalks and discard. Remove tips; set aside. Cut remaining stalks into 1-inch pieces and cook in boiling water for five minutes adding the asparagus tips the last two minutes. Drain and add to bowl of pasta. Add the chopped ham, shredded mozzarella cheese, corn, artichokes with marinade, olives and Parmesan cheese. Toss lightly. To make dressing: Thin the mayonnaise with milk and stir in mustard and Parmesan cheese. Pour over pasta salad and toss gently to coat. Makes 6-8 servings; serve warm or cold.

## Lime Meringue Pie

*Just like a lemon meringue pie only use limes instead of lemons.*

**9-inch Baked Pie Shell:**
1 cup all-purpose flour
¼ teaspoon salt
½ cup (1 stick) unsalted butter, chilled
2 tablespoons ice water

**Pie Filling:**
1 cup sugar
⅓ cup cornstarch
1 tablespoon tapioca
Pinch salt
2 cups boiling water
4 egg yolks, lightly beaten

*Continued on page 130.*

❖ *Pasta Salad* ❖

129

*Lime Meringue Pie continued from page 129.*

1 tablespoon butter
Zest of one lime (about 2 teaspoons)
Juice of one lime (about 3 tablespoons)
1 or 2 drops of green food coloring

**Meringue:**
6 egg whites
½ teaspoon cream of tartar
½ teaspoon vanilla extract
Pinch salt
6 tablespoons sugar

To make pie shell: Sift flour and salt in a bowl. With a pastry cutter, work flour and butter together until it is coarse and crumbly. Gradually add the water, mixing pastry until it forms a ball. Wrap and chill 1 hour.

Preheat oven to 475 degrees. Roll out chilled pastry on a lightly floured surface and fit into a 9-inch pie plate. Turn under excess pastry and crimp. Prick sides and bottom of pie pastry with a fork. Bake for 8-10 minutes. Set aside.

To make pie filling: In a small saucepan, combine sugar, cornstarch, tapioca, salt and boiling water and cook, stirring frequently, until thick, about 10 minutes. Remove from heat. Stir ½ cup of thickened cornstarch mixture into the beaten egg yolks, then add to remainder of cornstarch mixture stirring to blend. Return to low heat, add butter and cook, stirring constantly, for five minutes. Stir in lime zest, juice and food coloring; mix well. Set aside.

Turn oven to 350 degrees. To make meringue: Beat egg whites until fluffy. Add cream of tartar, vanilla and salt. Beat for 6 to 8 minutes or until stiff, adding sugar 1 tablespoon at a time.

Pour warm filling into baked pie shell. Spread meringue over filling, sealing to pastry edge and mounding into peaks. Bake 12 to 15 minutes until meringue is lightly browned. Cool 3-4 hours before cutting. Makes one 9-inch lime meringue pie.

❖ *Lime Meringue Pie* ❖

❖ *Carolina Peach Pie* ❖

# THEME PARTIES

2003 James Bond Party

*T*heme parties are great fun to host *and they tend to be informal which delights most guests. At the End of Summer theme parties, which Gene and I hosted for our school's 12-month staff, many guests got into the spirit of the theme by dressing accordingly (see photos). The themes varied from location themes; Hawaii (1991), Jersey Shore (1994) and Route 66 (1997) to entertainment themes such as Motown (2001), Looney Tunes (2001) and Westerns (2002). Gene and I created amusing names for menu items based on each theme and printed them on the party invitation. For example, the baseball theme party menu included "Piazza Pizza", "Diamondback Ribs" and "Anaheim Angels Food Cake with Darrell Strawberries". A theme trivia quiz was later added with a prize awarded to the winner with the most correct answers. A selection of these fun theme parties follows with some of the recipes served.*

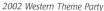

2002 Western Theme Party

1998 Baseball Theme Party

## CAROLINA FRUIT PIES

*Homemade pies were the signature dessert for the End of Summer parties. Fresh fruit was in season and readily available at the local farmers' markets. The top crusts were varied for an attractive presentation and vanilla ice cream was served on the side. The pies were usually arranged on a separate table allowing guests to sample at their leisure. (See photo on opposite page.)*

### *Carolina Peach Pie*

**Basic Pastry:**

2 cups all-purpose flour

$\frac{1}{4}$ teaspoon salt

1 cup (2 sticks) unsalted butter (save 1 tablespoon for greasing pie plate)

$\frac{1}{4}$ cup ice water

**To Assemble:**

Pie fillings (recipes follow)

1 tablespoon butter, cut into pieces

1 large egg, lightly beaten

To make pastry: Toss flour and salt in food processor. Add butter, cut into pieces, and pulse on and off until mixture resembles coarse meal. Gradually add ice water and

process briefly (20 seconds) until pastry leaves sides of bowl and forms a ball. Wrap in waxed paper and refrigerate an hour.

Preheat the oven to 400 degrees. Divide dough into two pieces. Lightly flour a flat surface and roll out dough into a circle to fit a 9-inch pie dish with a 1-inch overhang. Repeat with other piece of dough and use as a top crust or lattice top. Spoon in your choice of pie filling (recipes follow), dot filling with pieces of butter and cover with top crust. Turn pastry overhang under and crimp edges. Brush top crust with beaten egg and bake 50 minutes or until light brown. Makes one 9-inch pie. To make lattice top: Roll out dough and cut into strips. Lay pastry strips across top of pie in one direction leaving a $\frac{1}{4}$-inch space between strips. Peel back every other strip, to center of pie and lay additional strips in the other direction, going over and under the first strips. Crimp edges; brush top with egg; bake as directed above.

### Peach Pie Filling

8 cups peaches, peeled and sliced

$1\frac{1}{2}$ cups sugar

$\frac{1}{2}$ cup quick-cooking tapioca

$\frac{1}{4}$ teaspoon cinnamon (optional)

Toss sliced peaches with sugar, tapioca and cinnamon; fill a 9-inch pastry-lined pie plate. Bake as directed above.

*Pies pictured below, clockwise from top center: Apple, Blackberry, Cherry, Peach, Blueberry*   *1994 Jersey Shore Theme Party*

## Blueberry Pie Filling

4 cups blueberries

$\frac{1}{4}$ cup quick-cooking tapioca

$1\frac{1}{4}$ cups sugar

$\frac{1}{4}$ teaspoon each cinnamon and nutmeg

Dash salt

Toss berries with tapioca, sugar, cinnamon, nutmeg and salt. Fill a 9-inch pastry-lined pie plate. Bake as directed on opposite page.

*1994 Party*

**For blackberry filling:** Use 5 cups berries, 2 cups sugar, $\frac{1}{3}$ cup tapioca, $\frac{1}{4}$ teaspoon cinnamon, dash salt.

## Apple Pie Filling

6 cups Granny Smith apples, peeled, sliced

3 tablespoons flour

1 cup sugar

$\frac{1}{2}$ teaspoon cinnamon

Dash salt

Toss apples with dry ingredients and fill a 9-inch pastry-lined pie plate. Bake as directed in pie recipe on opposite page.

**For cherry pie filling:** Thaw and drain 4 cups pitted tart red cherries; reserve 1 cup juice. Cook juice with $\frac{1}{2}$ cup tapioca, $1\frac{1}{4}$ cups sugar and dash salt until thick. Add 1 tablespoon butter and $\frac{1}{4}$ teaspoon almond extract. Cool; stir in cherries; fill and bake (see page 134).

## ROUTE 66 PARTY

*In 1997, the theme for the End-of-Summer party was Route 66. The menu was a blue plate special often found in the diners that lined the road from Chicago to LA. It consisted of meat-loaf and gravy (recipe on page 74), piled high with crispy onion rings (recipe below), mashed potatoes and green beans with creamy cole slaw on the side. This down-home comfort food is hard to resist.*

### Fried Onion Rings

3 sweet onions, sliced ¼-inch thick
2 eggs, lightly beaten
½ cup milk
1 cup all-purpose flour
1 cup bread crumbs
Salt and pepper to taste
Oil for frying

Separate the sliced onions into individual rings. Arrange three shallow bowls on your work surface. Mix the eggs and milk in first bowl, flour in the second and bread crumbs in the third bowl.

Fill a large skillet with oil to about a half-inch depth and heat to 350 degrees. Dip onion rings, two or three at a time, first in the egg-milk mixture, then in the flour. Dip again in the egg-milk mixture and coat with the bread crumbs. With a pair of tongs, lower coated rings into the preheated oil and fry on both sides until golden brown. This will only take about a minute. If they brown too quickly, lower the temperature of the oil about 10 degrees. Drain on paper towels; season with salt and pepper and keep warm in the oven. Repeat with rest of onion rings. Serves 4-6.

❖ *Blue Plate Special* ❖

# BASEBALL TRIVIA QUIZ
*August 7, 1998*

**1. Who is credited with inventing baseball?**

   A. Strom Thurmond, who in 1875, was already in his sixties when he invented the national pastime.

   B. Abner Doubleday, who with a name like Abner, had to come up with something big.

   C. Yogi Berra, who much like Confucius, invented many clever sayings.

   D. Ken Starr, who as even President Clinton observed, can really play hardball.

**2. What active baseball player is fifth all-time in walks received?**

   A. Ricky Henderson, currently playing for the Oakland A's.

   B. Raol Mondisi, currently playing for the Dodgers.

   C. Nicky Novicky, one of the first Polish-Americans to make it to the Bigs.

   D. Wade Boggs, who really made out in the Bigs.

**3. The only pitcher to serve up 50 home runs in a single season was**

   A. Robin Roberts, who pitched for the Phillies.

   B. Al Downing, who also served up Hank Aaron's record-breaking home run.

   C. Burt Hooten, known for his knuckleball.

   D. Burt Blyleven, who pitched for Minnesota.

**4. How many double stitches are there in a baseball?**

   A. 190

   B. 109

   C. 901

   D. It varies depending on the country in which it is made and the amount of "juice" inside the ball.

**5. Who holds the record for the most home runs in a single season?**

   A. Mark McGuire, known as "Big Mac".

   B. Babe Ruth, known as "The Bambino".

   C. Roger Maris, known as Roger Maris.

   D. Davey Lopes, a well-known thief.

**6. Who holds the record for the most runs-batted-in for a single season?**

   A. Willie Mays, famous for his basket catches.

   B. Dolf Camilli, famous for his basket weaving.

   C. Bill Veck, famous for bringing in a midget to pinch hit in a major league game.

   D. Hack Wilson, famous for a nagging cough which persisted throughout his career, hence his nickname.

**7. The last year an American team won the Little League World Series.**

   A. 1908, also the last time the Cubs won the Major League World Series.

   B. 1927, the year the Yankees won the Major League World Series.

   C. 1988, the last year the Dodgers won the Major League World Series.

   D. 1993, a good year for California wines.

**8. For the first time in history, Major League Baseball has officially retired a player's number for all teams. What player was honored by this action?**

   A. Larry Doby, the first African-American to play in the American League.

   B. Jackie Robinson, the first African-American to play in the National League.

   C. Babe Ruth, acclaimed by many as the best player of all time.

   D. Pete Rose, who said 42 was his lucky number and he always bet on it.

**9. In scoring a baseball game, what number is assigned to the catcher?**

   A. 2, the square root of the average SAT score for catchers.

   B. 6, selected because it is the traditional lucky number for catchers.

   C. 4, derived by counting the positions in sequence beginning with the manager and first base coach.

   D. 9, determined by rank ordering positions by level of skill needed to play there.

**10. Which of the following was NOT inducted into the Baseball Hall of Fame this year?**

   A. Don Sutton, who played in the majors for 23 years.

   B. Larry Doby, who played for the Indians.

   C. Pete Rose, who bet his career he would make it.

   D. Lee McPhail, who was general manager of the Yankees.

*Answers: 1-B, 2-A, 3-D, 4-B, 5-A, 6-D, 7-D, 8-B, 9-A, 10-C.*

# BASEBALL PARTY

*There was a lot of fun material for the 1998 baseball theme party. Gene and I enjoyed creating the menu items (see box on right). The food, of course, resembled ball park eats: chili dogs (recipe follows), corn dogs, pizza, as well as fried chicken, ribs (recipe on page 94) and baked beans. Many guests dressed in their favorite teams' paraphenalia and arrived ready to test their knowledge with the baseball trivia test on the opposite page.*

*Step Up To The Plate*
*Friday, August 7, 1998 at 7 p.m.*
*Headmaster's House*

Piazza Pizza • Giants Shrimp
Dodger Dogs with Cincinnati Reds Hot Chili
Diamondback Ribs
Harry Carey Corn Dogs with Miami Marlin Mustard
Texas Free Ranger Chicken
Chicago Cub Club with Mariners Mayo
Cooperstown Cole Slaw • Boston Braves Baked Beans
Anaheim Angels Food Cake with Darrell Strawberries
Boston Cream Pie with Padres Pudding

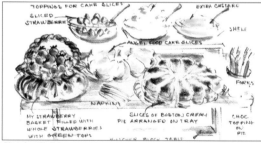

*Menu-Planning Sketches*

❖ *Chili Dogs* ❖

## CHILI DOGS

3 tablespoons olive oil, divided
1 pound ground beef
1 large onion, chopped
½ green or red pepper, chopped
1 can (15 oz.) tomato sauce
1 can (15 oz.) diced tomatoes, undrained
1 can (15 oz.) Northern or kidney beans,
    drained and rinsed
1 tablespoon chili powder
1 teaspoon salt
½ teaspoon garlic powder
1 teaspoon ground cumin
1 or 2 tablespoons sugar
¼ teaspoon bottled hot sauce
Optional garnishes: shredded cheddar
    cheese and sour cream
8 hot dogs and buns

Heat two tablespoons of oil in a large heavy skillet or Dutch oven pan and brown beef until no longer pink. Remove from heat and drain on paper towels. In same skillet, sauté chopped onion and pepper in one tablespoon of oil until soft. Add rest of ingredients and browned beef; bring to a boil. Reduce heat and simmer, uncovered, for one hour. Use as topping for grilled hot dogs on a bun or serve in bowls topped with cheddar cheese and sour cream. Serves 6-8.

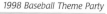
*1998 Baseball Theme Party*

# MAYBERRY PARTY

*Southern food is comfort food, especially in the small town of the fictional Mayberry R.F.D. popularized by the television series. To plan the menu for our theme party, Gene and I made a special trip to Mt. Airy, North Carolina, the real town upon which Mayberry was based. The general store provided lots of party props and ideas for the menu. "Andy" Pasto (recipe follows) and "Aw Gee, Paw" Cheese Ball started the Mayberry evening followed by "Nothing Could Be Finer" Carolina Cornbread (recipe follows), and Aunt Bee's "Bless Her Heart" Fried Chicken. See menu on right for more details.*

**PDS Staff and Administrators' Party**
*At Mayberry R. F. D.*
**Saturday, August 14, 1999 at 7 p.m. Headmaster's House**
●

Aw Gee, Paw Cheese Ball • "Andy" pasto
Aunt Bee's ("Bless her heart") Fried Chicken
Barney Fife's Deputy Dogs with Hot Plate Chili
Floyd's Favorite Ribs with Barbershop Barbecue Sauce
Extry Good Potato Salad • Goober's Beanie Salad
Carolina's Corn Pone ("Nothing could be finer")
Country Bumpkin Pumpkin Pie
Blueberry Pie with Opie's Oreo Cookie Ice Cream
Aunt Bee's ("Bless her heart") Blue Ribbon Apple Pie
Clara's Cuckoo Coconut Cake (If you're cuckoo for coconut, this cake's for you.)
Goober's Radiator Flush Punch and other Mayberry Specialty Drinks

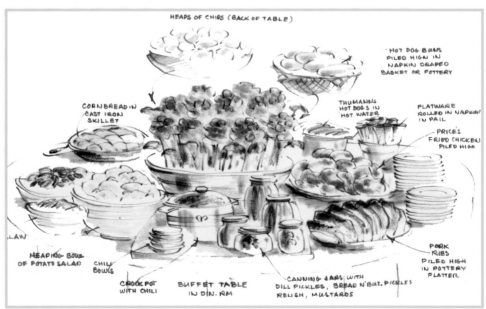

*Table Sketch*

❖ *"Andy"Pasto* ❖

## ANTIPASTO

1 eggplant, unpeeled
Salt, to taste
2 red or yellow peppers
2 tablespoons olive oil
1 ring of pepperoni, sliced
1 jar (10 oz.) marinated artichokes, drained
Assorted olives
Additional olive oil, for drizzling

Cut eggplant into ¼-inch slices; salt and stack slices. Let sit for 10 minutes, then blot eggplant slices on paper towels, brush with oil and grill until browned on one side. Arrange overlapping slices on a serving platter. Cut peppers in half and remove seeds. Drizzle oil over pepper halves, place skin side down on the grill and cook until skins are blistered. Remove from grill and peel skins from peppers. Arrange on serving platter with grilled eggplant. Add pep-peroni slices, artichokes and olives in rows on platter. Drizzle with additional olive oil and serve. Serves 4 to 6 as an appetizer.

## *Carolina Cornbread*

1 teaspoon canola oil
2 cups yellow corn meal
½ cup all-purpose flour
¼ cup sugar
1½ teaspoons baking powder
½ teaspoon salt
2 eggs, lightly beaten
1 can (14¾ oz.) cream-style corn
½ cup buttermilk
¼ cup canola oil

Preheat oven to 400 degrees. Brush a 9-inch oven-proof pan with one teaspoon of oil; set aside. Mix all dry ingredients in a large bowl; set aside. In another bowl, mix all liquid ingredients together and pour into the bowl of dry ingredients. Stir just until blended; do not over mix. Bake in preheated oven for 30 minutes. Cool and slice into wedges. Serves 8 to 10.

❖ *Carolina Cornbread* ❖

❖ *Blueberry Hill Cobbler* ❖

# MOTOWN PARTY

*On August 5, 2000, our guests arrived to the sounds of the 50's and 60's, courtesy of Gene's 45-record collection. Fats Domino, Bo Diddly, Gladys Knight and The Pips also lent their names to the dishes that were served: The Big Bopper's Biscuits, Bo Diddly's Baked Ham Jive with Diana's Maybe Baby Gravy, the Pips' Black-eyed Peas, the Coasters' Yackety Yak Yams, wrapping up with Shoo Be Doo Be Doo Da Desserts: Fats' Blueberry Hill Cobbler (recipe below) and Jumpin' Jack Flash Fresh Peach Cobbler.*

## *Blueberry Hill Cobbler*

**Filling:**

4 cups fresh blueberries

1 1/2 cups sugar

3 tablespoons cornstarch

1/2 cup water

2 tablespoons butter

**Pastry:**

1 cup all-purpose flour

1/4 teaspoon salt

1/2 cup (1 stick) unsalted butter

2 tablespoons ice water

1 tablespoon butter, for filling

1 tablespoon sugar, for sprinkling

To make blueberry filling: Mix blueberries, sugar, cornstarch, 1/2 cup water and two tablespoons of butter in the top of a double-boiler. Cook, stirring frequently, until mixture thickens. Set aside.

To make pastry: Toss flour and salt together in a bowl; cut butter into pieces and work into flour until mixture resembles coarse meal. Stir in two tablespoons of ice water until mixture forms a ball. Wrap in plastic wrap or waxed paper and chill for one hour in the refrigerator.

Preheat oven to 400 degrees. Remove pastry from refrigerator and roll out on a floured surface into a circle large enough to line a 9-inch deep-dish baking pan with a one to two-inch overhang. Butter the baking pan and line with the rolled-out pastry. Add cooked blueberry filling, dot with tablespoon of butter cut into pats and fold pastry overhang partially over the filling. Sprinkle with the tablespoon of sugar and bake in preheated oven for 25 to 30 minutes until pastry is golden brown. Spoon warm cobbler into dessert dishes and add a dollop of vanilla ice cream to each dish. Serves 6.

# WESTERN PARTY

*For the Western theme party, many of the old cowboy and cowgirl stars of the black-and-white television era came to mind and the menu items reflected those characters. We served Gabby Hayes Ham and Tex Ritter Red-Eye Gravy, Hopalong Hoppin' John (recipe follows) with Roy Rogers Rawhide Steak, Annie Oakley's Onion Rings, Stagecoach Sourdough Biscuits and Marshall Matt Dillon Dill Pickles.*

## Hoppin' John

*The traditional recipe for Hoppin' John, which is usually made on New Year's Day and thought to bring luck, involves soaking dried black-eyed peas in water overnight and then cooking with a ham bone or ham hock for flavoring. Substituting frozen black-eyed peas and a ham slice speeds up the cooking process with no loss in taste.*

2 tablespoons olive oil
1 medium onion, chopped
1 cup long grain rice
1 bag (16 oz.) frozen black-eyed peas
$\frac{1}{4}$ teaspoon red pepper flakes
1 can (14.5 oz.) chicken broth
6-ounce slice ham ($\frac{1}{2}$-inch thick), cubed

Heat oil in a Dutch oven pan and sauté the chopped onion until soft and translucent. Stir in the rice and coat with the oil, then add the frozen black-eyed peas, pepper flakes and chicken broth. Bring to a boil. Reduce heat and simmer for 20 minutes until rice and peas are tender. Add cubed ham the last five minutes of cooking time. Serves 6 as a side dish.

*Western Theme Party, August 3, 2002*

148

❖ *Hoppin' John* ❖

❖ *Black Caviar Canapés* ❖

# "007" THEME PARTY

*Bond was back with a cast of characters for the End of Summer Party held on August 23, 2003. Guests delighted in the slightly salty taste of the "To die-for" Black Caviar Canapés (recipe follows). And it was no secret that "Q's" secret ingredient for his Classic Caesar Salad with Cool Capers was the Cartel's recipe for croutons. Furthermore, it was no surprise that Money Penny's Pasta (recipe follows) would ring up a winner in the taste department. No secret agents were detected in the crowd gathered around the dessert table, but one guest was overheard to remark, "You Only Live Twice, so eat dessert first!"*

## Black Caviar Canapés

**Cheese Spread:**

2 packages (3 ounces each) cream cheese, room temperature

$\frac{1}{4}$ cup sour cream

**Egg Spread:**

$\frac{1}{4}$ cup chopped celery

$\frac{1}{4}$ cup chopped green onion, white and green parts

4 hard-boiled eggs, shelled and quartered

$\frac{1}{4}$ cup mayonnaise

Salt and pepper, to taste

**For Canapés:**

18 slices (1-pound loaf) firm white sandwich bread, crusts removed

4 ounces black caviar, drained

To make cheese spread: In an electric mixer, beat softened cream cheese and sour cream until smooth, 1-2 minutes; set aside.

To make egg spread: In a food processor, pulse celery and green onion until minced. Add eggs and mayonnaise; pulse until mixed well. Set aside.

To prepare bread slices: Moisten a clean tea towel and lay on a cutting board, anchoring one end of towel at top of board. Arrange 4 bread slices in the upper half of moist towel then fold bottom of towel over bread slices. With a rolling pin, flatten bread to about an $\frac{1}{8}$-inch thickness. Set aside between two tea towels to keep moist and repeat process with rest of bread.

To make stacked canapés: Spread the cream cheese filling on one flattened bread slice, top with a second bread slice and spread with egg mixture. Add a third slice of bread, spread with cheese filling, then a fourth slice with egg filling. Top with a fifth bread slice and spread with cheese filling. Wrap stack in aluminum foil and refrigerate for at least three or four hours to firm up bread and spreads. (This will allow for easier cutting into canapés.) Repeat process with 5 additional bread slices and spreads; wrap and refrigerate.

*Continued on page 152.*

*Black Caviar Canapés Continued from page 151.*

To make rolled-up canapés: Spread a layer of cheese filling on a flattened bread slice, then spread a layer of egg filling right on top of cheese layer. Roll up from long end of slice removing excess filling and sealing edge. Repeat with rest of flattened bread slices and spreads. (You should have 8 rolled-up logs.) Wrap in aluminum foil and refrigerate for 3 or 4 hours.

To assemble stacked canapés: Remove the two 5-layered stacks from refrigerator and place on a cutting board. Trim rough edges of four sides of one of the stacks, then make 2 slices across horizontally at 1-inch intervals and then across vertically. This will make 9 one-inch squares. Sprinkle with caviar and arrange on a tray. Repeat with other layered stack. Refrigerate until ready to serve. Makes 18 square, stacked canapés.

To assemble rolled-up canapés: Remove 8 rolled-up "logs" from refrigerator and place on a cutting board. Trim rough edges off both ends and make two slices across at 1-inch intervals. This will make 3 canapés from one log. Repeat with rest of logs. Stand upright and sprinkle tops with caviar and arrange on a tray. Refrigerate until ready to serve. Makes 24 round, rolled-up canapés.

## PENNE PASTA

*To keep with the "007" theme, we called this recipe "Money Penny's Pasta". It is a quick and easy dish to make and can be made ahead and refrigerated. Just bring it back to room temperature before serving.*

4 ounces penne pasta
1 teaspoon olive oil
3/4 pound large shrimp, cooked, shelled and deveined
4 fresh Roma tomatoes, peeled, seeded and chopped
1/4 cup chopped green onions (green and white parts)
4 ounces Feta cheese, crumbled
1 tablespoon freshly chopped oregano or 1 1/2 teaspoons dried oregano

Cook the pasta according to the manufacturer's directions; drain and toss with olive oil. Set aside.

In a large bowl, combine the shrimp, chopped tomatoes, green onions, feta cheese and oregano. Add cooked pasta and toss until well blended. Serve with crusty bread. Serves 4.

❖ *Penne Pasta* ❖

❖ *Tangerine French Toast* ❖

## CHRISTMAS BREAKFASTS

*Dec. 2000*

*ᴇ̃ach holiday season, Gene and I hosted a Christmas breakfast for our administrative staff. It usually took place right before the holiday break from school when the weather had turned cold and everyone was getting into the holiday spirit. Gene and I did our best to hasten that along. We decorated the Christmas tree, hung the wreath on the door and played Christmas carols on the CD player. We made sure the fireplace was lit to warm our guests as they arrived at our door.*

*The challenge for me each year was to create a breakfast menu for 10 to 12 people that could be served hot and could be enjoyed by all the guests at the same time. Over the years, I managed to find and adjust recipes that could be prepared a day ahead, at least partially, and then finished in the oven the next morning. A selection of breakfast recipes appears in this section, starting with Tangerine French Toast which was served at the 1999 Christmas breakfast.*

*December 18, 2003*

*December 19, 2000*

# TANGERINE FRENCH TOAST

*This French toast recipe is great for serving a large group for breakfast. The tangerines can be glazed the day before and the French toast is baked in the oven. This recipe serves four people, but it can be doubled or tripled for additional servings.*

**Glazed Tangerines:**

4 tangerines

1/2 cup orange marmalade

2 teaspoons water

**Cranberry Syrup:**

1/4 cup cranberry juice

1/2 cup pure maple syrup

1/3 cup fresh cranberries

1/2 teaspoon orange extract

**French Toast:**

Juice from one tangerine, about 1/4 cup

4 large eggs

1/2 teaspoon orange extract

8 slices Italian bread

Unsalted butter, for baking sheets

Optional garnish: fresh mint leaves

To make Glazed Tangerines: Peel the skin off the tangerines and carefully remove the white pith. In a small saucepan, heat the orange marmalade and water until it starts to simmer. Continue to simmer for about 5 minutes stirring to mix the marmalade and water into a syrup. Remove from heat and dip tangerines into the syrup, coating all sides. Place glazed tangerines in a container, cover and set aside or refrigerate.

To make Cranberry Syrup: Combine cranberry juice, maple syrup, cranberries and extract in a saucepan and heat to a simmer. Continue to simmer until cranberries are cooked but do not burst, about 10 minutes. Keep warm until ready to use.

To make French toast: Preheat oven to 425 degrees. Heat a large baking sheet on the stovetop with about two tablespoons of butter until the butter has melted. Mix the tangerine juice, eggs and orange extract in a shallow baking dish until well blended. Dip the bread slices in the mixture until both sides are completely coated and arrange on the buttered baking sheet. When all of the slices have been dipped and placed on the baking sheet, transfer to the preheated oven. Bake about five minutes, turn slices over and bake an additional five minutes or until golden brown.

To serve: Place two slices of French toast on each of four plates. Add a glazed tangerine garnished with some of the cooked cranberries from the warm syrup and a fresh mint leaf. Serve with warm cranberry syrup. Makes 4 servings.

# ❖ *Shirred Eggs* ❖

## *Shirred Eggs*

*This egg recipe was served for the 2004 Christmas breakfast. It is very easy to make for a large group, but you will need individual shallow baking dishes for each serving.*

2 cups shredded Swiss cheese

16 eggs

8 tablespoons milk

Salt and pepper, to taste

Preheat the oven to 350 degrees. Butter eight individual shallow baking dishes and sprinkle the bottom of each baking dish with $\frac{1}{4}$ cup of shredded cheese. Carefully break two eggs into each baking dish without breaking the yolks. Spoon one tablespoon of milk over the eggs and season with salt and pepper.

Place filled baking dishes on a cookie sheet and bake in preheated oven for 15 minutes. Serve in the baking dishes or lift out with a spatula and serve on a plate. Serves 8.

### ❖ *Banana Crepes* ❖

# BANANA CREPES

*These crepes can be made with almost any fresh fruit and complementary jam or jelly. For the 2003 Christmas breakfast, I prepared an assortment of crepes: blueberries and jam, raspberries and jam and bananas and jam. By far the favorite was the banana crepes. The crepe pancakes can be made a day ahead, cooled and stacked between waxed paper and refrigerated. The next morning, bring to room temperature, fill, wrap, heat in the oven and serve. How easy is that!*

**Crepe Batter:**
2 cups milk
2 cups all-purpose flour
1 tablespoon sugar
4 eggs, separated
2 tablespoons melted butter
Unsalted butter, for brushing skillet and
    tops of filled crepes

**Crepe Filling:**
Banana jam (available in specialty shops)
8 to 10 bananas

**Garnishes:**
Banana slices, strawberries, green grapes
Confectioners sugar

    Beat milk, flour, sugar and egg yolks until well blended. Whisk the egg whites until foamy with soft peaks; fold into batter and stir in melted butter.

    Heat an 8-inch, nonstick frying pan over medium heat and brush lightly with unsalted butter. Lift pan from heat and ladle about $\frac{1}{4}$ cup of batter into pan turning to spread the batter around into a thin crepe. Cook over medium heat on one side only for about $1\frac{1}{2}$ minutes; turn out onto paper towels. Repeat with rest of batter. If you're making the crepes the day before serving, layer crepes between sheets of waxed paper or plastic wrap on a plate; cover with plastic wrap and refrigerate.

    The next day, remove crepes from refrigerator and bring to room temperature. Preheat oven to 325 degrees. Spread crepes with banana jam; slice bananas and line several slices down the center of each crepe, than roll and place in an ovenproof shallow baking dish. Brush tops of filled crepes with additional melted butter and warm in the preheated oven for 10 minutes. Serve with garnishes. Makes 20 filled crepes, about two crepes per person.

# CUSTARD FRENCH TOAST

*In this recipe, French bread slices are soaked in a creamy custard overnight, then simply baked in the oven the next morning. I served it at the 1997 Christmas breakfast with lots of blueberries, raspberries and strawberries.*

1 loaf French bread, cut into 1-inch slices
½ cup sweetened dried cranberries
8 large eggs
1 pint heavy cream
Dash salt
1 teaspoon vanilla
¼ cup light brown sugar
½ teaspoon cinnamon
Dash nutmeg
Garnishes: orange slices, fresh berries

Arrange bread slices tightly in a buttered 13x9-inch baking pan; sprinkle with cranberries. Mix eggs, cream, salt, vanilla, brown sugar and spices until well blended. Pour over bread pressing slices down into custard. Cover with heavy aluminum foil wrapped tightly around edges of baking dish. Refrigerate overnight.

The next morning, remove from refrigerator and let stand at room temperature about 30 minutes. Preheat oven to 350 degrees. Bake for 35 minutes. Remove the foil and return to the oven for 5 minutes. Cut into squares and serve, bottom-side up, on individual plates. Garnish with fresh orange slices and berries and serve with maple syrup. Serves 10.

❖ *Custard French Toast* ❖

160

## QUICHE CUPS

*For the 2005 Christmas breakfast, a basic quiche filling was baked in crepe-lined muffin tins. Red and green fruits garnished the plates.*

**Crepes:**

2 large eggs

1 cup milk

1 cup all-purpose flour

$\frac{1}{4}$ teaspoon salt

2 tablespoons melted butter

Butter, for brushing pan

2 six-cup jumbo muffin pans

**Quiche Filling:**

6 large eggs

$1\frac{1}{2}$ cups heavy cream

$1\frac{1}{2}$ cups half and half

Pinch salt, pepper and nutmeg

1 cup grated Gruyere cheese

1 cup diced ham

1 tablespoon butter, cut into pieces

Additional grated Gruyere cheese

To make crepes: Beat eggs; add milk, flour, salt and melted butter. Beat until smooth. Set aside for 30 minutes. Heat an 8-inch non-stick pan and brush with butter. Pour $\frac{1}{4}$ cup batter into pan and swirl around to spread batter evenly. Cook on one side only for less than a minute. Fit uncooked side down

into a buttered muffin cup. Repeat with rest of batter. If making a day ahead, cover loosely with plastic wrap and refrigerate.

To make quiche filling: Preheat oven to 350 degrees. Whisk eggs with cream, half and half, salt, pepper and nutmeg. Sprinkle cheese and diced ham over bottom of each crepe cup and fill with egg mixture to $\frac{1}{8}$ inch from top. Dot with butter and additional cheese. Bake 25 minutes until custard is firm. Remove from muffin pans and serve. Makes 12 quiche cups.

❖ *Quiche Cups* ❖

161

*Parsippany, NJ*　　　　　　　　　　　　　　　　　　　　　　　　　　　*June 4, 1994*

*Photograph by Dian Brownfield*

**O**n a lovely day in June, *our son Jim married his college sweetheart, Tara Malooly. Much to my delight, they both love to cook and entertain friends in their home. Tara has introduced me to hummus and baba ganoosh, recipes she enjoyed as a child. The learning and searching never stops. Whether exploring new countries and foreign dishes, meeting new people and new cultures, or enjoying a new chapter in our lives, we are constantly "searching for watercress" and for success in the kitchen.*

*Lake Norman, NC　　　July 3, 2002*

162

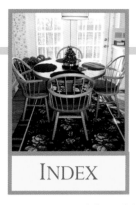

# INDEX

## A

Almond Coffee Ring, 75
Antipasto, 144
Apple(s)
    Baked, 13
    Pie Filling, 135
    Strudel, 38
Asparagus and Ham Roll-ups, 27

## B

Baked Apples, 13
Baked Fennel, 119
Baklava, 107
Banana Crepes, 159
Barbecued Spare Ribs, 94
Barbecues and Cookouts, 93
Baseball Party, 139
Beans
    Black-eyed Peas, in Hoppin' John, 148
    Green, Southern-style, 71
    Green, yellow, and kidney, in
        Three Bean Salad, 71
    Northern or Kidney, in Chili, 141

Béchamel Sauce, 111
Beef. See also Steak
    Meatloaf, 74
    Sauerbraten, 36
    Stew, 21
Blackberry Pie Filling, 135
Black Caviar Canapés, 151
Blueberry
    Hill Cobbler, 147
    Pie Filling, 135
Bologna Roll-ups and Stacks, 25
Bread
    Carolina Corn, 144
    French, Homemade, 102
    Walnut, 65
Breaded Veal Cutlet (*Wiener Schnitzel*), 34
Bride's Dinner, 13
Brie en Croute, 84
Brunswick Stew, 97

## C

Cabbage
    Red, 36
    Stuffed, 62

Caesar Salad, 104
Cake(s)
   Almond Coffee Ring, 75
   Chocolate Cheese Mini-Cup-, 52
   Chocolate Train, 51
   Pound, 76
   Red Velvet, 79
Canapés, Black Caviar, 151
Candy Cookies, 83
Carolina Cornbread, 144
Carolina Fruit Pies, 134
Cheese
   Blue, Dip, Crudités and, 89
   Brie en Croute, 84
   Cheddar
      And Potato Pierogies, 61
      And Capers, Ham Squares
         with, 26
   Cream
      Chocolate, Mini-Cupcakes, 52
      Filling, for Grape Tarts, 121
      Icing, for Red Velvet Cake, 79
      In Black Caviar Canapes, 151
      In Bologna Roll-ups & Stacks, 25
      In Prune and Nut Crescent
         Cookies, 66
      In Salmon & Cucumber Stacks, 26

Feta
   In Greek Salad, 120
   Penne Pasta with, 152
Gruyere, in Quiche Cups, 161
Mozzarella, in Manicotti, 115
   See also below under Parmesan
      with Mozzarella.
Parmesan
   And Gruyere, in Chicken Pinwheels,
      110
   Caesar Salad with, 104
   In Baked Fennel, 119
   In Béchamel Sauce, 111
   In Dressing, Iceberg-Romaine Salad,
      126
   With Mozzarella
      And Fontina, in Spinach Lasagna, 111
      And Ricotta, in Lasagna, 48
      In Mushroom & Sausage Frittata, 112
      In Pasta Salad, 128
Ricotta
   With Mozzarella, in Manicotti, 115
   And Parmesan, in Lasagna, 48, 111
Swiss, in Shirred Eggs, 157
Cherry Pie Filling, 135
Chicken
   Hunter Style, 31

Chicken (Cont.)
   In Brunswick Stew, 98
   In Paella, 118
   In Wine (*Coq au Vin*), 17
   Kiev, 105
   Pinwheels, 110
Chili Dogs, 141
Chocolate Cheese Mini-Cupcakes, 52
Chocolate Train Cake, 51
Christmas Breakfasts, 155
Christmas Party, 87
Clams, in Paella, 118
Cobbler, Blueberry Hill, 147
Cookies
   Candy, 83
   Gingerbread, 54
   Painted, 57
   Prune and Nut Crescent, 66
Cookies & Milk Party, 83
*Coq au Vin* (Chicken In Wine), 17
Cornbread, Carolina, 144
Crab Cakes, 123
Cream Puffs, Mini, 53
Crepes
   Banana, 159
   Pasta, for Manicotti, 115
Crudités and Blue Cheese Dip, 89
Custard French Toast, 160

**D**

Desserts. See specific dessert.

Dip, Blue Cheese, Crudités with, 89
Dressing. See Salad Dressing.
Duck, Roast, 15

**E**

Eggs
   In Mushroom & Sausage Frittata, 112
   In Quiche Cups, 161
Eggs, Shirred, 157
Egg Spread, in Black Caviar Canapés, 151
Eggplant
   In Ratatouille, 72
   In Antipasto, 144

**F**

Faculty Luncheons, 108
Fennel, Baked, 119
First Cocktail Party, 23
Flank Steak, Rolled, 87
French Bread, Homemade, 102
French Toast
   Custard, 160
   Orange, 44
   Tangerine, 156
Fresh Pumpkin Pie, 67
Fried Okra, 71
Fried Onion Rings, 136
Fried Squash, Southern, 18
Frittata, Mushroom & Sausage, 112
Fruit. See specific fruit.

## G

Garden Vegetables, 71
German Potato Salad, 31
Gingerbread Cookies, 54
Grape Tarts, 121
Greek Salad, 120
Green Beans, Southern-style, 71

## H

Ham Squares with Cheddar &
  Capers, 26
Headmaster's Dinner, 102
Holiday Pastries, 65
Homemade French Bread, 102
Hoppin' John, 148
Hors d'oeuvres
  Asparagus & Ham Roll-ups, 27
  Black Caviar Canapés, 151
  Bologna Roll-ups & Stacks, 25
  Ham Squares with Cheddar
    & Capers, 26
  Pickle Roll-ups, 26
  Salami & Watercress, 27
  Salmon & Cucumber Cream
    Cheese Stacks, 26
  Tuna Roll-ups, 24
Hunter Style Chicken, 31

## I

Iceberg and Romaine Salad, 126

## Icing

Cream Cheese, for Red Velvet Cake, 79
For Almond Coffee Ring, 75
For Gingerbread Cookies, 54

## L

Lasagna, 48
  Spinach, 111
Lime Meringue Pie, 129
Low Country Grill, 93

## M

Manicotti, 115
Mayberry Party, 142
Meatloaf, 74
Mini-Cream Puffs, 53
Motown Party, 147
Mushroom & Sausage Frittata, 112

## O

Okra, Fried, 71
Onion(s)
  Rings, Fried, 136
  Stuffed Vidalia, 96
"007" Theme Party, 151
Orange French Toast, 44
Orange Sauce, for Duck, 15
Oven-baked Pancake, 45
Oven-roasted Potatoes, 123

*P*

Paella, Seafood, 118
Painted Cookies, 57
Pancake(s)
    Oven-baked, 45
    Smiley Face, 43
    Zucchini, 47
Party(-ies)
    Barbecues & Cookouts, 93-95
    Christmas, 87-90
    Christmas Breakfasts, 155-161
    Cookies & Milk, 83
    Faculty Luncheons, 108-115
    First Cocktail, 23
    Headmaster's Dinner, 102-107
    PTO Luncheon, 90-92
    Theme, 133-153
        "007", 151
        Baseball, 139
        Mayberry, 142
        Motown, 147
        Route 66, 136
        Western, 148
    Trustee Socials, 117-131
    Wine & Cheese, 84-85
Party Hors d'oeuvres, 22
Pasta
    Crepes, for Manicotti, 115

Lasagna, 48
Penne, 152
Salad, 128
Spinach Lasagna, 111
Pastry
    Basic, for double-crust pie, 134
    Crust, for Grape Tarts, 121
    For Cobbler, 147
    For 9-inch Baked Pie Shell, 129
Peach & Pineapple Squares, 69
Peach Pie, Carolina, 134
Pickle Roll-ups, 26
Pierogies, 61
Pie(s)
    Carolina Fruit, 134
        Apple, Blackberry, 135
        Blueberry, Cherry, 135
        Peach, 134
    Fresh Pumpkin, 67
    Lime Meringue, 129
Pink & Green Social, 128
Pork
    Barbecued Spare Ribs, 94
    Sausage
        Frittata, Mushroom and, 112
        In Low Country Grill, 93
        In Potato Soup, 32
        In Rolled Flank Steak, 87
        In Seafood Paella, 118
        In Stuffed Vidalia Onions, 96
        In Tomato Sauce, for Lasagna, 48

Pork Tenderloin
    In Brunswick Stew, 97
    With Baked Apples, 13
    With Pineapple, 126
Potato(es)
    And Cheddar Cheese, in Pierogies,
      61
    In Low Country Grill, 93
    Oven-roasted, 123
    Salad, German, 31
    Soup, 32
    Sweet, Mashed, 13
Pound Cake, 76
Prune and Nut Crescent Cookies, 66
P.T.O. Luncheon, 90
Pumpkin Pie, 67

## Q

Quiche Cups, 161

## R

Ratatouille, 72
Red Cabbage, 36
Red Rice & Ribs, 94
Red Velvet Cake, 79

Ribs, Barbecued Spare, 94
Rice
   *Coq au Vin* with, 17
   In Hoppin' John, 148
   Paella with, 118
   Savannah Red, 94
Roast Duck, 15
Rolled Flank Steak, 87
Route 66 Party, 136

## S

Salad
   Caesar, 104
   Greek, 120
   Iceberg and Romaine, 126
   Pasta, 128
   Potato, German, 31
   Spinach, 89
   Three Bean, 71
Salad Dressings
   For Caesar Salad, 104
   For Iceberg and Romaine Salad,
     126
   For Pasta Salad, 128
   For Spinach Salad, 89
   Vinaigrette, for Greek Salad, 120

Salami & Watercress Hors d'oeuvres, 27
Salmon and Cucumber Cream Cheese Stacks, 26
Sauce
    Béchamel, for Spinach Lasagna, 111
    Cream, for Seafood Strudel, 90
    Orange, for Roast Duck, 15
    Seafood Cocktail, for Low Country Grill, 94
    Tomato, for Lasagna, 48
        For Spinach Lasagna, 111
Sauerbraten, 36
Savannah Red Rice, 94
Seafood Cocktail Sauce, 94
Seafood Paella, 118
Seafood Strudel, 90
Shirred Eggs, 157
Shrimp
    In Low Country Grill, 93
    In Paella, 118
    In Penne Pasta, 152
    In Seafood Strudel, 92
Smiley Face Pancakes, 43
Soup, Potato, 32
Southern Fried Squash, 18
Southern-style Green Beans, 71
Southern Trifle, 98
Spareribs, Barbecued, 94
Spinach
    Lasagna, 111
    Salad, 89

Spring Buffet 2001, 123
Squash
    Canoes, 18
    In Ratatouille, 72
    Southern Fried, 18
    Zucchini Pancakes, 47
Steak
    Flank, Rolled 87
    Flank, in Brunswick Stew, 98
Stew
    Beef, 21
    Brunswick, 97
Strudel
    Apple, 38
    Seafood, 90
Stuffed Cabbage, 62
Stuffed Vidalia Onions, 96
Sweet Potatoes, Mashed, 13
Syrup
    Cranberry, for Tangerine French Toast, 156
    For Baklava, 107

## T

Tangerine French Toast, 156
Tarts, Grape, 121
Theme Parties, 133-153
Three Bean Salad, 71
Tomato Sauce, 48, 111
Train Cake, Chocolate, 51
Trifle, Southern, 98

Trustee Socials, 117-131
Trustee Social 2003, 125
Tuna Roll-ups, 24
Turkey
   Sausage
      Frittata, Mushroom and, 112
      In Low Country Grill, 93
      In Potato Soup, 32
      In Rolled Flank Steak, 87
      In Seafood Paella, 118
      In Stuffed Vidalia Onions, 96
      In Tomato Sauce, for Lasagna, 48

## V

Veal, Breaded Cutlet, (*Wiener Schnitzel*), 35
Vegetables. See specific vegetable.
Vidalia Onions, Stuffed, 96

Vinaigrette Dressing, for Greek
   Salad, 120

## W

Walnut Bread, 65
Watercress, Salami and,
   Hors d'oeuvres, 27
Western Party, 148
*Wiener Schnitzel*, (Breaded Veal Cutlet), 35
Wine & Cheese Party, 84

## Z

Zucchini
   In Ratatouille, 72
   Pancakes, 47
   Southern Fried, 18

# CREDITS

Food Preparation and Food Photography: Rose Marie Bratek
Food Tasting and Photographs of Author: Gene Bratek
Photographs of Family and Friends: Rose Marie and Gene Bratek
Recipes Edited by: Sally McNeill, RD, Nutritionist

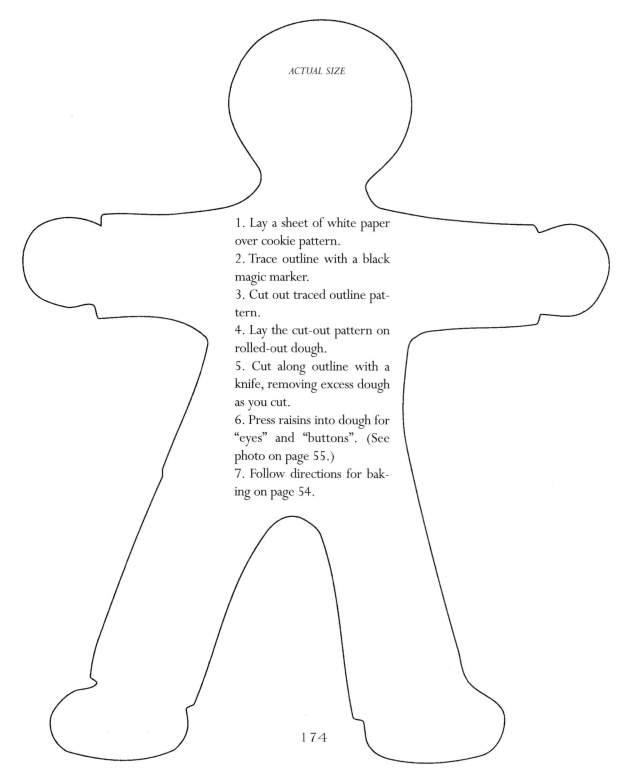

*ACTUAL SIZE*

1. Lay a sheet of white paper over cookie pattern.
2. Trace outline with a black magic marker.
3. Cut out traced outline pattern.
4. Lay the cut-out pattern on rolled-out dough.
5. Cut along outline with a knife, removing excess dough as you cut.
6. Press raisins into dough for "eyes" and "buttons". (See photo on page 55.)
7. Follow directions for baking on page 54.

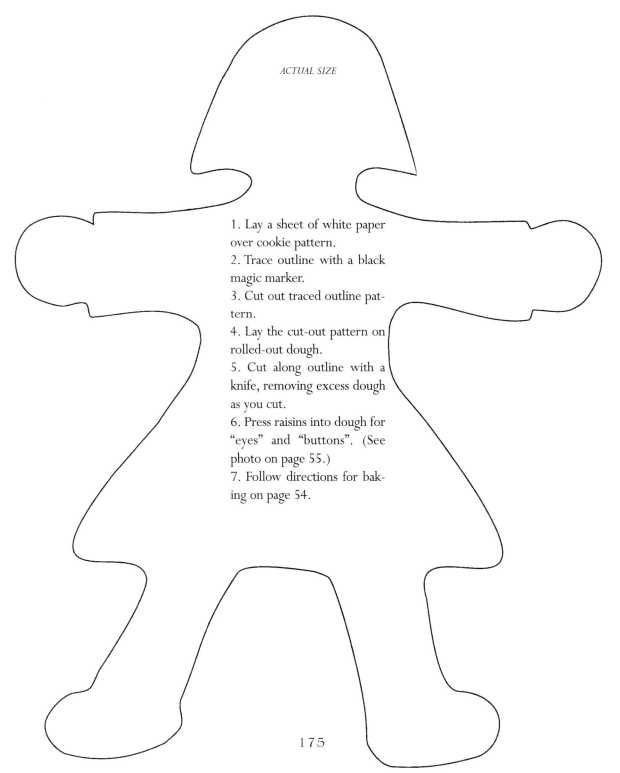

*ACTUAL SIZE*

1. Lay a sheet of white paper over cookie pattern.
2. Trace outline with a black magic marker.
3. Cut out traced outline pattern.
4. Lay the cut-out pattern on rolled-out dough.
5. Cut along outline with a knife, removing excess dough as you cut.
6. Press raisins into dough for "eyes" and "buttons". (See photo on page 55.)
7. Follow directions for baking on page 54.